Norfolk At War
1939–45

Dedication

This book is dedicated to Dr Ming-yu Tseng with thanks for all his help and support.

Norfolk At War 1939–45

Stephen Browning

Pen & Sword
MILITARY

First published in Great Britain in 2018 by
PEN & SWORD MILITARY
An imprint of
Pen & Sword Books Ltd
47 Church Street
Barnsley
South Yorkshire S70 2AS

Copyright © Stephen Browning, 2018

ISBN 978 1 47385 699 8

Printed and bound in England
By CPI Group (UK) Ltd, Croydon, CR0 4YY

Typeset in Times NR MT by SRJ Info Jnana System Pvt Ltd.

Pen & Sword Books Ltd incorporates the Imprints of
Atlas, Archaeology, Aviation, Discovery, Family History, Fiction, History, Maritime, Military, Military Classics, Politics, Select, Transport, True Crime, Air World, Frontline Publishing, Leo Cooper, Remember When, Seaforth Publishing, The Praetorian Press, Wharncliffe Local History, Wharncliffe Transport, Wharncliffe True Crime and White Owl.

For a complete list of Pen & Sword titles please contact
PEN & SWORD BOOKS LIMITED
47 Church Street, Barnsley, South Yorkshire, S70 2AS, England
E-mail: enquiries@pen-and-sword.co.uk
Website: www.pen-and-sword.co.uk

Contents

Dedication		ii
Acknowledgements		vii
Introduction		ix
Chapter 1	1939	1
Chapter 2	1940	32
Chapter 3	1941	82
Chapter 4	1942	125
Chapter 5	1943	194
Chapter 6	1944	241
Chapter 7	1945	293
Appendix 1 Norfolk Airfields in the Second World War		305
Bibliography		309
Index		311

Acknowledgements

I am grateful to the excellent website www.roll-of-honour.com which is run by volunteers and to whom any financial contribution is very welcome – see site. The following individuals have transcribed material which has been of especial interest in this study: Martin Edwards (Downham Market, Alburgh, Upper Sheringham, Runcton Holme); Steve Smith (Hemsby, Ormesby); Chris Basey (Acle, Hemblington); Carolynn Langley (Burnham Market, Burnham Westgate, Burnham Sutton and Burnham Norton, Cley, Thornham, Burnham Overy, Snettisham, Hunstanton St Edmunds, Castle Acre, Swaffham, Worstead Holt) and Lynda Smith (Fleggburgh St Margaret and Billockby, Diss, Burnham Overy, Hunstanton, Burnham Market, Burnham Westgate, Burnham Sutton and Burnham Norton, Aldeby, Cley, Snettisham, Worstead, Swaffham, St Edmunds, Holt, Brancaster, East Ruston, Mundesley, Castle Acre); Claire Langley (Holt); David Rudram (Mundesley); Ernie Rusdale (Hunstanton St Edmunds); Raymond Harvey (Forncett St Mary); Rosemary Browne (Great Yarmouth Civilian Dead); Chris Clarke (Wymondham); Geoff Sewell (Aldeby, Worstead); Mick Tilley (Alburgh); Peter Dearsley (Weeting); Brian Lees (Tacolneston); Stuart McLaren (Norwich St Augustine); Ray Goddard (Diss); Rosalind Hoffmann (Chedgrave); Lucy Hall (Fleggburgh St Margaret and Billockby).

I am also indebted to R. Douglas Brown for one of the great feats of Norfolk historical scholarship – his seven volume account of East Anglia 1939–45. The books are sadly out of print at the time of writing but I managed to buy a complete set from several different second-hand bookshops.

Local newspapers and magazines of the period have been consulted extensively and thanks go to the custodians of these priceless sources of information. I have also used social media from time to time, notably Facebook, to appeal for information from Norfolk citizens about their family members who served in the war or in appeals for details of specific features or actions of the conflict. The often gratifying and interesting results are included in the text.

It is always a pleasure to deal with staff in Norfolk libraries. Thank you. I have also researched some rare papers for this book in the British Library in London and this has been very rewarding: thanks to the professional and friendly staff.

Photographs come from many different archives, newspapers, periodicals, government sources and official war photographers. Some fine shots have recently been released into the public domain by the Imperial War Museum. I am grateful to top Norfolk photographer, Daniel Tink, for permission to reproduce some of his work www.danieltink.co.uk. Daniel also has a nationally-known site of East Anglian images which are available for sale www.scenicnorfolk.co.uk. Unless otherwise indicated, all present-day photographs are by the author.

At Pen & Sword I would like to thank my commissioning editor, Roni Wilkinson, for all his excellent advice and Janet Wood for editing the book and making valuable suggestions.

Introduction

This is the first study yet published to give a detailed, year-on-year narrative account of Norfolk during the years 1939-45.

There are some interesting books that approach the Second World War in Norfolk from different angles, maybe in themes or pictures. There are also some fascinating studies of particular aspects of the conflict such as the role of the USAAF or the so-called 'Baedeker Blitz'. These books are given in the Bibliography.

However, in bringing the war to life, month on month and contrasting the mood of the people of Norfolk at, say, the beginning and the end of any year it is hoped this account presents the war in the way it was actually seen and felt by the people of Norfolk. Through a succession of fascinating times and events such as Churchill's 'sinister trance', The Battle of Britain, Dunkirk, the incredible feats of the RAF, the USAAF, the coastal communities and ships, the sufferings of Norfolk's men in Singapore and Burma, the key role of the county's troops on D-Day and beyond, and through to eventual Allied victory we can trace the 'slings and arrows of outrageous fortune' as it affected the people of Norfolk. This, the greatest drama ever told, had its fluctuating high and low points, its humour, and stories of heroism and tragedy as well as everyday problems, and these are presented as they happened.

Life at home is extensively covered – homes, prices, shopping, food, ideas, restrictions on movement, the Home Guard, entertainment, changing laws, the courts, accommodating thousands of Italian prisoners, coping after the bombs, welcoming refugees both from London and the Norfolk coast, becoming accustomed to the continuous noise of overhead aircraft engines, seeing the land transformed by huge engineering projects to build airfields, the change to social norms when tens of thousands of the county's menfolk were not around and women coped triumphantly when given new roles from farming to manning the searchlights as the V1s approached with their distinctive hum followed by a harsh rattle, and, not least, the enormous difference that the arrival of thousands of Americans made to the county.

Honour is paid to the deeds of the men and women who gained great distinction in battle, as well as the many more who did not make the history books and civilians who suddenly lost their lives in bombing raids. A small section at the end of each year gives the names and details of a small number of people from Norfolk who gave their lives in the conflict. It is intended by giving the names of a few to honour the many.

There are over 300 photographs and charts specially selected from many sources to bring the narrative to life.

CHAPTER ONE

1939

At A Glance: Local and World events

JANUARY

Local

Extreme weather experienced in Norfolk – snow and storms. Civil Defence Volunteers recruited. National Service Committees meet. Lists of accommodation for school evacuees begin: Jewish children arrive.

World

General Franco storms Barcelona. Prime Minister and Foreign Secretary meet with Mussolini in Rome.

FEBRUARY

Local

Warmer weather comes to East Anglia. Much discontent among farmers leads to march and rally in Westminster, London. East Anglia finances ship of food for Spain.

World

General Franco's government is recognized by leading nations, including Britain and France.

MARCH

Local

Work continues on cataloguing addresses for potential evacuees and building shelters. Territorial Army ups recruiting campaign. Fire and explosion at Great Yarmouth power station. School hockey and football team exchanges continue with Germany.

World

Spanish Civil War ends with Franco triumphantly entering Madrid. Germany occupies Czechoslovakia. Polish independence guaranteed by Great Britain. Territorial Army put on war footing.

APRIL

Local

Bright weather. Recruitment stepped up for armed forces. Home defence exercises take place all over East Anglia. German hockey team hosted by Ipswich.

World

Germany refutes Polish treaty and Anglo-German Naval Treaty. Italy occupies ports in Albania. Britain increases Defence budget and introduces six month conscription for men aged 20. Britain announces creation of Ministry of Supply and Women's Land Army.

MAY

Local

Talks held throughout county to consider best use of hospitals. Airfields in Norfolk hold Air Days to show off planes. Weather encourages people to flock to seaside.

World

British King and Queen visit Canada and America. Soviet Union proposes pact with Britain and France. British farmers promised £2 per acre subsidy for ploughing new land and a guaranteed price for some crops including oats and barley: inventory of ploughs and tractors undertaken.

JUNE

Local

Royal Norfolk Show held at Diss. Fundraising drives initiated for hospitals. Harwich hosts destroyers and minesweepers. Hunstanton Pier destroyed by fire.

World

British government increases payments for certain crops such as oats and barley and guarantees financial security for voluntary hospitals. Some 200,000 conscripts sign up in Britain.

A Sergeant instructs two men in the use of a rifle, probably an M1917 Enfield.

Houses in Cathedral Close, Norwich, 1939 and today.

JULY

Local

Norfolk takes part in secret and large-scale RAF exercises, along with seventeen other counties. Good trade reported at coastal resorts.

World

In Britain the first conscripts report for duty.

AUGUST

Local

Huge mock air attack on East Coast. Black-out exercises over East of England. Holiday makers flock to the seaside. Deep sea trawlers ordered to return to port. Norfolk hospitals told to make plans for receiving potential casualties from London.

World

In Britain the Emergency Powers (Defence) Bill passed and plans drawn up for identity cards. Non-aggression pact is signed between Germany and Russia. British Ambassador in Germany meets Hitler.

SEPTEMBER

Local

Evacuees received all over Norfolk; trenches dug for shelters; air raids expected but do not materialize. War committees take over essential agricultural and coastal tasks; ploughing of waste land encouraged. U-boats and mines sink ships off coast.

World

In Britain, expectant mothers and children begin evacuation from London. Petrol rationed. War declared and general mobilization.

OCTOBER

Local

Traders on the coast hold meeting to discuss their special problems.

World

Conditions at Buchenwald concentration camp published. In Britain, Ministry of Food begins centralized control of all aspects of livestock rearing; a quarter of a million men sign up.

NOVEMBER

Local

Germany mines East Coast with consequent loss of shipping.

Air raid drill at Norwich School.

World
Hitler survives attempted assassination in Munich beer hall.
Rationing introduced in Britain.

DECEMBER

Local
Blackout restrictions relaxed in places.

World
Soviet Union expelled from League of Nations.

> *In the bleak mid-winter*
> *Frosty wind made moan,*
> *Earth stood hard as iron,*
> *Water like a stone;*
> *Snow had fallen, snow on snow,*
> *Snow on snow,*
> *In the bleak mid-winter*
> *Long ago.*

Christina Rossetti (c1872)

A bitter winter

January 1939 was bitterly cold. Five inches of snow fell on Great Yarmouth in a single day and Norwich recorded 18.8 degrees of frost. On the coast the fishermen battled with ships encased in ice. A wet mist fell on top of the snow. Whole villages turned out with shovels in a desperate attempt to clear the snow before it melted.

Worse was to come in the form of exceptionally heavy rainfall, Ipswich in Suffolk recording 2½ inches on 25 and 26 January. All over Norfolk rivers began to burst their banks and homes were flooded: furniture and all sorts floated along some streets. The weather was the worst since the Great War.

The population of East Anglia as a whole in 1939 – the land of the East Angles, consisting of Norfolk, Suffolk and Cambridgeshire – was about 1.7 million, less than a third of that today. Norfolk accounted for 529,000 of those with slightly more females than males. The largest settlement and only city was Norwich where just over 118,500 people lived (today that figure is just over 132,000, although that figure grows to about 290,000 for the 'greater' Norwich area) and, of the towns, Great Yarmouth housed just over 50,000 people, King's Lynn about 26,000 while several – Cromer, Hunstanton, Thetford,

A tale of two City Halls: at the back of the photograph is the 'new' City Hall, building on which stopped in 1938. The building of knapped flint in the foreground is 500 years older – the clock is a Victorian addition.

Sheringham and Diss – were communities of around 4,000. Thus, at the beginning of 1939, the majority of Norfolk folk lived in small rural settlements scattered over this huge, at times inhospitable, landscape.

It is fair to say that Norwich was an important centre in 1939, but the rest of the county seemed remote in some respects from national affairs. Even the resorts like Cromer and Great Yarmouth which catered for hundreds of thousands of visitors every summer drew most of their trade from northern cities and East Anglia itself, not from London and the South East. Norfolk was famously 'not on the road to anywhere else' and some people even considered that the railway network, being

Sheringham panorama showing wide-open beach. (Daniel Tink)

limited and unreliable, did more to cut off the county than open it up to outsiders. The locals travelled little, maybe to the nearest market town occasionally or to the coastal villages for a holiday each summer. To many, London was almost a foreign country.

The Great War had been a shock to many areas of Britain but less so to much of Norfolk. There had been some incursions by Zeppelins with tragic loss of life and the German fleet had attempted a noisy pummelling of Gorleston and Yarmouth with farcical results. For the first half of the conflict, at least, the greatest fear was of an invasion on the Norfolk coast but this mercifully did not materialize. Norwich did not suffer any serious attack whatsoever. Many in Norfolk felt that the conflict could have been a lot worse. The county's young men, however, paid a terrible price and this resulted in, for some time at least, women taking over jobs and responsibilities traditionally associated with men-folk. But then things calmed down, the old order gradually reasserted itself and by 1939 the Great War seemed a very long time ago, almost as if it had not occurred at all.

Agriculture remained the largest employer, engaging about 30 per cent of men, while much of the huge estates were owned by titled landowners like the Duke of Grafton. The landed gentry came next in the social scale and they gave employment to the workers. In between was a growing middle class – bankers, well-to-do farmers, shopkeepers and teachers: a reasonable salary may have been about £250 per year with a bonus at Christmas, and some would aspire to send their boys to the top private school in the county – Norwich Grammar School. Upward social mobility was no longer the impossible dream it once was.

Pre-war disasters in 1939

There were several major fires in East Anglia in 1939. On Saturday night, 11 June, a crowd of 15,000 gathered to watch as a fire gutted the end part of Hunstanton Pier, the blaze being visible for 30 miles. On 27 July the East Anglian School of Painting and Drawing at Dedham, Essex was lost along with its irreplaceable art library. St Mary's Baptist Church, Norwich, was completely lost to fire after morning service on 10 September.

There were two serious railway accidents. On Whit Monday five coaches of the Cromer to London train left the track at Witham: luckily no-one was badly injured. On 31 May a Hunstanton to London train collided with a lorry near Dereham, killing four women.

A giant rat caused a short-circuit in the power station in Great Yarmouth in March with one set of paws on one terminal and the other on another 10 inches away. Great Yarmouth and parts of Lowestoft were blacked out for a while. One employee was killed and five injured. Another short-circuit, for reasons unknown, caused Norwich Corporation power station to fail in July – the whole city and a large area of surrounding countryside were affected.

Housing before the war

If you were in a position to buy your own house, exactly as today the cost varied according to where you decided to live. To give some idea of the market, a detached four-bedroomed bungalow or house in the country or small town would cost perhaps about £500. If you wanted to live in a better part of Norwich, the local press of 1939 shows that this amount would buy you possibly a good three-bedroomed terrace property with garden or a two/three bedroomed semi-detached house with garden. A large detached residence of say six bedrooms in an acre of ground – much as you can find today in the so-called 'Golden Triangle' of Norwich – would be between £1,500 and £2,000. In 2018 such properties changed hands for upwards of £750,000. A thriving farm of 50 acres plus house would be £2,000 or more.

Most people could not afford to buy and rented either from their employer or local authorities; many lived in accommodation that went with the job, so-called 'tied' cottages. There was, in addition, a thriving private renting business – then, as now, if you had a substantial amount of spare cash, by investing in the property market you could simultaneously play 'safe' and also gain a good return. A one-bedroomed flat in Norwich would command about £80 a year upwards (in 2018 terms this figure equates to about £7,000). In the country villages and small towns, the same amount would rent you a semi-detached house with a reasonable garden.

The Great War had shone a light on the often poor health of the recruits from Norfolk and this, in turn, highlighted a poor (and often drunken, in some areas at least) lifestyle and a desperate housing situation. Many rented properties, especially tied ones, were appalling with no sanitation, heating or water. Sometimes, on account of a rat invasion, it was necessary to move all foodstuffs upstairs but, if this was the case, rats still came into bedrooms at night. In the towns and Norwich things were hardly better, although it was easier to lay on electricity and sanitation here if the money could be found. Norwich cleared over 4,000 slum properties in the 1930s and made a start on what was hoped would be a housing revolution with a great housing estate at Earlham. In the same period, Swaffham ordered the destruction of 150 cottages whilst, on the advice of the Medical Officer of Health, 300 houses in the Downham Market district were declared unfit for human habitation.

The problem was not that people did not know what needed to be done, but, as ever, money. As regulations came into force for standards to be enforced – on water, sanitation, ventilation and so on – so the costs of improving sub-standard accommodation grew. This affected both huge landowners such as the Duke of Grafton and individual farm owners who were having a very thin time financially anyway.

Jobs, pay, shopping and prices

We know how much people earned in considerable detail because of a survey by Cambridge University into manual labour which reported in July 1939. A typical wage for agricultural workers was 35 shillings a week (there were 20 shillings to the pound). Top of the list in regards of pay was work in clothing or printing at 60 shillings a week. In between were the other jobs available in Norfolk – brush, clothing and furniture making, food and drink production and engineering. Of particular importance was boot and shoe making in Norwich which, during the Great War, had produced literally several million pairs of marching boots of unsurpassed quality for the allied armies, and which was still a booming sector in 1939. Jobs were generally plentiful and rates of pay 58 shillings a week for men and 38 shillings for women as the war began, and this was to increase by several shillings for both sexes before the year was out. The reasons given for the disparity in pay between men and women were size of hands, physical strength and likely length of service. There was much talk in the papers about equal pay for equal work but, in Norfolk as a whole, the situation was very little changed from thirty years before.

Norwich as a whole was prosperous and jobs not difficult to find. Colman's employed 2,500 down on Riverside (as it is named today where the site of the old factory is now luxury flats). Their most famous product was mustard but they also produced starch and washing blue. Today the firm has shunted a short way along the river and thrive as a part of the Unilever conglomerate. Boulton & Paul, in the same area, had produced more of the famous Sopwith Camel aircraft than anyone else during the previous conflict, one of which had been responsible for the death of the famous Red Baron, Baron von Richthofen, scourge of British flyers. They thrived still although the order book now featured mostly steel construction projects. Also in the area was Laurence, Scott & Electromotors.

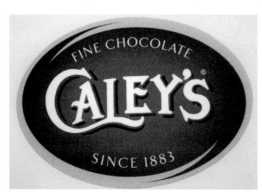

A famous Norwich brand of chocolate, still available.

Back in the town centre and on the present site of Chapelfield Shopping Centre was A.J. Caley & Son who, during the previous conflict, had produced millions of slabs of the famous Caley's Marching Chocolate which were sent as gifts to the Norfolk Regiment on the front. It can still be bought in the city today. Perhaps the most famous firm of all was the Norwich Union Life Insurance Company, now renamed AVIVA, which had developed from a principally commercial insurance company to one that served almost every aspect of the general population.

Women were in demand for domestic service, especially in Norfolk: 58 per cent were thus employed in the county as opposed to 35 per cent in the nation as a whole.

The picture was not wholly bright. Some of the traditional Norfolk industries were in decline – clothing, including corset making, mat and brush making and even the mainstay shoe production of Norwich which was to see a catastrophic decline in the late 1970s. Docks such as King's Lynn were vulnerable to the disruption caused by international uncertainties. However, the coming of war seemed, at least initially, to reduce unemployment a little. Some areas, however, suffered badly and this is borne out by the famous story of the Czechoslovak refugees who, once billeted along the East Coast, put on concerts to raise money for their hosts.

As regards stores, one of the most famous and still thriving today, was Jarrold & Sons. Another was R.H. Bond which was later bought by the John Lewis group: it was celebrating its diamond jubilee as the war broke out and it employed over 200. Eddingtons was another where ladies of means would drop by and hand in their shopping list, remaining seated whilst the assistant gathered everything together. There was a Marks & Spencer and a Woolworths which had the slogan 'Nothing over sixpence'. Most towns also had a Montague Burton where suits for men were around 45 shillings and, as everyone wore hats, a fine display of everything from bowlers to caps to fur-lined 'winter warmers'.

Butter was 1s 6d per lb; the famous Colman's mustard 8½d per ¼lb tin; strawberry jam 9d per lb jar; cheddar cheese 1s per lb; sausages 1s 4d per lb; sugar 4½d per lb; apples 1s per lb; and ground coffee 1s 8d per pound. There was no shortage of

Chapelfield Gardens, central Norwich, had been a training ground for troops since Agincourt and was used by the newly-formed Home Guard.

demand for more luxurious foodstuffs. Lobster was 1s 6d a tin; Turkish delight about the same as lobster; a good port about 6s; a bottle of whisky or gin about 14s.

For the home, a dining room suite would be £14 upwards whilst a twenty-six-piece dinner-service could be yours for about 10s upwards; a piano would retail at about 24 guineas (1 pound and 1 shilling equalled 1 guinea) and an HMV automatic radiogram cost 15 guineas. Very few people could entertain owning a television but some splashed out the incredible sum of £12 and upwards for a radio. Telephones were becoming indispensable – the present exchange in St Andrews Street in Norwich dates from this period.

Then as now, the motor car was one of the ultimate symbols of affluence. This was the heyday of some names that have almost vanished – Hillman, Austin, Wolseley, Binder and Riley. Rolls-Royce were at this time producing cars for everyman, one of their open topped 40/50 h.p. models retailing at around £145.

In comparison, Ford sold their smaller cars at about £115 and
a Hillman Minx was around £175. A common sight as the war
progressed was to see a car painted on one side in a camouflage
of woodland or bricks so as to blend in when parked: this cost
about 35 shillings.

Hospitals and doctors

The role of the state in looking after the health of the population was very limited. Major hospitals, such as the Norfolk
and Norwich, had Contributors' Associations – in 1939, for example, £37,300 from a total outlay of £68,000 was raised by
people paying 2p per week. The hospital made a loss even then
and had a waiting list of 800. Every avenue was tried to raise
funds – dances, clay pigeon shoots, football games, bring-and-
buy sales, village tug-of-war contests and so on.

If you chose, you could go for treatment to a private hospital
but the cost would be upwards of 10s a day, a very great deal
of money to most people. Some contributed to Friendly and
Temperance societies which had a medical officer. A system
of medical insurance had been patchily introduced from 1911
and the government worked with various societies such as the
Rechabites or the Oddfellows. Burial Clubs operating from the
1500s had broadened their remit and taken on new names in
order to offer limited medical services to their members.

Lack of nourishment for many in the county, along with
lack of hygiene, meant going without a meal in the daytime, no
baths and, in many areas, complete family infestation of fleas
and ticks.

Education

The school leaving age was just fourteen and the war postponed
a planned raising of this to fifteen. Most learnt little more
than basic reading, writing and limited mathematics. Norwich,
however, was rapidly advancing in educational provision in
1939 – a new school for 500 boys was opened in Catton and

Chamberlins in their pomp, occupying extensive premises just off Norwich Market Place.

the first nursery school in Norfolk was constructed in Earlham. A new technical college, authorized to confer degrees, was proposed for Norwich. Whilst not denying that manifold problems needed to be overcome, there was a feeling that we could be about to enter a new golden age of learning.

The Fishermen

The fishing industry had peaked just prior to the Great War and by 1939 had suffered a serious decline, the catch having halved in thirty years. Nonetheless a dozen settlements on the Norfolk coast still relied on the catch for their livelihoods. Apart from the fishing boats themselves there were jobs for several thousand women gutting and cleaning the fish and for a similar number of men curing, packing and transporting the catch. Then, of course, there was need for all manner of waterproof clothing which was something some large firms such as Chamberlins in Norwich had been providing in massive quantities in the 1914–18 war and since.

The Norfolk coast had traditionally been famous for the herring, the season for which was from the end of September to Christmas. Then there was mackerel and, once, plaice which had mysteriously all but disappeared in the 1930s. On 23 August 1939 the government requisitioned the trawlers on the East coast for war purposes – as minesweepers and auxiliary warships. It decided that 250 vessels might continue fishing but each fisherman had to obtain a special fishing permit which was authorized by the navy. This much-reduced fleet actually had a fine catch of herring which achieved the record price of 2d each, which was exactly double the price of the same fish on the port sides in 1914. Such was the glut that the Admiralty did its best to help by issuing a Fleet Order recommending increased use of herrings in naval diets.

Hotels and Guest Houses

The Great War had seen the bankruptcy of many seaside businesses as people cancelled bookings once hostilities had started or simply just failed to show up. This was a lesson that was not lost in 1939 as it became more and more likely that war was coming. A big campaign was launched by the London and North Eastern Railway Company in May to 'Meet the sun on the East Coast'. One hundred national and local newspapers were targeted with adverts and articles on the joys of Great Yarmouth's 130ft high Observation Tower, Cromer's fine air and Hunstanton's exceptional golf courses and bracing walks. Gorleston invested in a new Floral Hall for dancing and ambitious programmes for entertainments were publicized everywhere. Alas, the weather did not cooperate as cloud and rain descended: it was not until mid-August that sunshine came and by then it was too late to save the season for many local traders.

The Grand Hotel, Cromer, was one of several impressive establishments on the sea front. It was built in the 1890s and destroyed by fire in 1969. The site is now Albany Court flats.

Squadron Leader D.O. Finlay in front of his Spitfire MKIIA, 23 November 1940.

A Rush to War

'My good friends this is the second time in our history that there has come back from Germany to Downing Street peace with honour. I believe it is peace in our time.'

Prime Minister Neville Chamberlain

'I saw my enemies in Munich, and they are worms.'

Adolf Hitler

'An appeaser is one who feeds a crocodile, hoping it will eat him last.'

Winston Churchill

The preparations for war as 1939 progressed were unprecedented both in their scale and increasing speed. In early January the government decided that the size of the army was to be increased to six regular and twenty-six Territorial divisions. Aircraft production had a great deal to do if it was to catch Germany's output and orders were given to prioritize this almost irrespective of cost.

Second World War pillbox and lighthouse at Happisburgh. (Daniel Tink)

A Norwich family building an Anderson shelter – a sense of humour is evident as the wheeled toy animal looking down has been given a gas mask!

New airfields were given priority. At first, the main airfields in East Anglia were not in Norfolk but at Felixstowe, Martlesham Heath and Duxford. It was here that the Hurricanes – top speed 316 mph – and the Spitfires – top speed 355 mph – were developed and tested. Each had eight machine guns in contrast to the previous maximum of four on the Gladiator. Similarly, heavy bomber technology resulted in the Blenheims being able to carry 1,000lbs of bombs for 1,460 miles and the Wellingtons 4,500lbs for 1,200 miles.

A mass recruitment campaign was begun for the forces. The RAF had great success when they opened many airfields on Empire Day in May 1939 putting on a thrilling display which included Wellingtons, Hurricanes, Spitfires and Blenheims. Tens of thousands attended and thousands signed up. Various squadrons were 'adopted' by Norfolk towns. There was also what we would today call a very successful media campaign centred around George Formby's film *It's in the Air*: RAF personnel would attend the initial screening and talk to the audience.

The army also set about recruiting in a hurry. Since 1881 each county had recruited its own regiment with two battalions of infantry. From 1908 the Territorials were formed resulting in battalions of part-time volunteers. Specifically regarding Norfolk, the 2nd battalion of the Royal Norfolks returned from serving in Gibraltar in January 1939. A fourth battalion of Territorials was raised from Norwich, Yarmouth, Attleborough and Harleston and a fifth from Dereham, Aylsham, Holt and North Walsham. On 29 March, the government announced that the size of the Territorials was to be doubled and, next month, ordered the conscription of all men aged twenty to twenty-one.

Recruitment was swift, and in Norfolk the 4th, 5th and 7th battalions were brought up to strength and a 6th battalion was raised in Norwich.

The government turned its attention to shelters, many simple examples of which, built in 1938, were little more than trenches. It now said that shelters, with roofs, should be available for 10 per cent of the population. A major problem with most of these was flooding and many people abandoned them in favour of sheltering under the stairs or bed. Norfolk was already ahead of the game, however, as regards preparations: Norfolk Air Raid Precautions (ARP) Committee had, by January, enlisted 5,000 wardens and appointed four full-time ARP officers at salaries of £350 per annum – all were ex-Army officers. It was also training 2,902 volunteer casualty service workers.

On 31 July Norwich Education Committee authorized the sum of £37,000 to provide shelters for schoolchildren over eight years of age on the assumption that children below that age would remain at home. The growing sense of urgency, that a 'real war' was coming, was heightened in Norwich in this month by large scale Civil Defence exercises.

The first evacuees

By the time war broke out, an evacuation plan was ready, an assessment having been made in 1938 under the direction of Sir John Anderson. It was, however, controversial, not least because of the apparent arbitrary manner in which areas were deemed suitable for receiving evacuees. Norwich, for example, had not received much attention from Zeppelins in the Great War and yet it was deemed 'neutral' which meant unacceptable, whilst Ipswich, which had suffered badly, was given 'acceptable' status. Further fire was added to the argument when the government declined an offer by Richard Stokes, MP, to manufacture shells in his Ipswich factory being told that the area was too vulnerable for such activity.

However, evacuation began on Friday, 1st September when the first of 20,000 children arrived over four days at Thorpe Station in Norwich. Scouts and Guides helped put them all in buses which would take them to dispersal centres in nearby schools. Here they were given a quick inspection for lice and

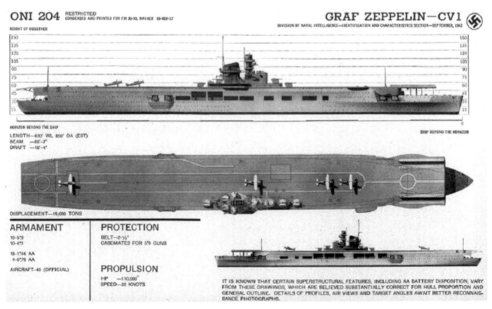

Representation of the Graf Zeppelin.

colds and each given a bag of rations containing one can of beef, milk, two small blocks of chocolate and a pound of biscuits.

Other children arrived on steamers which brought them from the Thames in London to Lowestoft, Great Yarmouth or Felixstowe.

Most evacuees were billeted with families in Norfolk villages, and often were moved again in a few days as conditions proved unsuitable: for instance, some secondary children from Bethnal Green in London were first sent to Aylsham in Norfolk only to find that there was no secondary school there and had to be re-routed to North Walsham. Another problem was that many only had clothes quite unsuitable to Norfolk winters, and much disagreement ensued as to who was responsible for the cost of equipping them.

Unsurprisingly, many quickly returned to London, especially the females: the pain of separating from close families was the most common given reason. Most, however, stayed, and the operation was deemed a success.

War is declared at last

War approached the consciousness of the people of Norfolk in a very slow fashion. There was muttering, there was talk and various scare stories but, on the whole, Norfolk people were, like the rest of the nation, caught up in what Winston Churchill called 'a wave of perverse optimism'.

Then, on Sunday 9 July came a combined RAF/Civil Defence exercise over 16,000 square miles of East Anglia and the south. It continued for three days and nights and involved simulated attacks by 500 bombers. This coincided with the reporting to barracks of the first conscripts. Shortly afterwards, the 18th East Anglian T.A. Division was sent to defend the coastal areas.

Frantic efforts were made to complete shelters, Norwich finally managing to construct enough for all schoolchildren over eight years of age by late November.

Early in August the *Graf Zeppelin* was tracked cruising off the East Coast. It was monitored by Radio Direction-Finding

Some areas of Norwich urgently needed modernising in the 1930s. This is King Street showing the sixteenth-century Ship Inn which was eventually purchased by the City Council in 1970 and turned into two houses.

King Street housing today.

(R.D.F.) stations which, in the east, were at Darsham, Stoke Holy Cross and West Beckham. Their effective tracking range was about 60 miles.

War was declared on 3 September, the declaration from the Prime Minister ending with the words: 'May God Bless you all. May He defend the right for it is evil things that we shall be fighting against – brute force, bad faith, injustice, oppression and persecution; and against them I am certain that right will prevail.' Two days later a combined Army, RAF and Navy recruiting centre was established in the Assembly Rooms and Agricultural Hall at Norwich. Soon, the British Expeditionary Force began to land in France, and this included the 1st battalion of the Suffolk Regiment and the 2nd battalion of the Royal Norfolks.

Apart from several raids, the main RAF activity in the early weeks was in dropping propaganda leaflets over Germany. At this time there were fifteen military airfields in East Anglia with four others under construction.

Changes to life at home: Problems with fish; Home Entertainments

The first essential job for everyone was to build shelters and blackout windows both at home and at work – a task by no means easy given that the Norfolk and Norwich Hospital alone had 1,600. Blackout material cost 3d per yard and not everyone could afford this. Ex-Army blankets rigged up on a sliding frame were an excellent alternative – if available. Some people went to extremes – one locally celebrated lady from Norwich who lived in a substantial house with wooden shutters to the windows, made sure they were OK to use and painted them all with country scenes, declaring 'I tried to copy John Constable.' In Norwich, the Bishop was one of the first to be prosecuted for showing a light, although to be fair this was someone in one of his rented houses, for whom he was responsible. The courts dealt with a variety of cases and issued fines ranging from a few shillings to three pounds. Those so convicted earned the name

The Guildhall, Norwich shored up and protected by sandbags.

The Guildhall and 'new' City Hall today.

the 'wish-bone group' having, according to their upstanding neighbours, wish-bones instead of backbones.

Bus and train services were cut back, especially in rural areas; newspapers became smaller to preserve newsprint; post office deliveries were reduced to two a day (there used to be considerably more); and people had to become used to carrying their own shopping home as shop staff signed up for the forces. Petrol rationing was re-introduced from 16 September with a single grade, called 'Pool', retailing at 1s 6d a gallon – this was increased next month to 1s 8d and by December it was 1s 10d. There were prosecutions for hoarding. People took to horses once again and the government was forced to remind everyone that, if you wished to attach a horse to a carriage then a licence was required, the cost increasing according to the number of animals attached.

Air raid sirens were not at first taken seriously as no planes or Zeppelins ever appeared.

The huge task of preparing lists for identity cards and ration books began – in Norwich this took up to 100 staff and volunteers who beavered away for ten days in City Hall. It was required that everyone register with retailers by 23 November and rationing was set to begin on 8 January 1940: each person was allowed twelve ounces of sugar, four ounces of bacon and four ounces of butter – soon the scheme was extended to include six ounces of any meat per head per day.

Worried about enemy attack on the coast, the government introduced a scheme for central distribution of fish. All fish was now to be taken to Norwich and the fish merchants had to follow it before taking the fish back to the towns and villages. An army of officials was needed and much stock was left to rot. After only a week the scheme was abandoned and sale of fish was resumed on the coast.

Entertainments carried on as much as was possible. Saint Andrews Hall in Norwich was blacked out and a series of classical concerts was staged. The Norwich players announced new productions for Christmas. As in the Great War people began to read more – W.H. Smith and Boots promoted a library service. Cooking demonstrations were popular.

On the coast

Activity of all kinds, including the saddest, took place along the East Coast. Several German airmen ditched into the North Sea and were drowned, their bodies being washed up: they were buried with military honours. The first such funeral was at Happisburgh where three men were buried but only two German flags could be found with which to drape the coffins.

Off the coast the war was a reality immediately. The first casualty to gain the attention of the press was the sinking of the merchantman *Magdapur* of 8,641 tons off Suffolk. The Aldeburgh lifeboat, *Abdy Beauclerk*, was sent out and rescued seventy men – this was the first of innumerable lifeboat rescues around the coasts of Britain.

Sinkings were common thereafter, German planes often dropping mines by parachute with the residents of the coastal towns lining the cliffs and promenades for a view of proceedings. The local press was not amused, pointing out that exactly the same foolhardy behaviour had been in evidence in the Great War. Had the coastal residents learned nothing? On 18 November the Dutch liner *Simon Bolivar* was sunk after hitting a mine off the Suffolk coast and three days later the Japanese liner *Terukuni Maru* was destroyed near Harwich – everyone on board was rescued. On the same day HMS *Gypsy* was mined with the loss of forty men. Over 65,000 tons of smaller shipping was sunk in a few days.

A remarkable feature of the earliest sinkings by U-boats was the behaviour of the combatants. In many cases the U-boat commander invited the British skipper on board for a meal. Sometimes a bottle of gin was given and, on occasions, even the ship's catch of fish was collected and sent to ashore. This did not last long, however, as tempers flared.

Some Norfolk Soldiers, Sailors and Airmen

William Herbert Henry Barrett, Able Seaman, Royal Navy, HMS *Rawalpindi* on 23 November 1939, aged 31. His ship was sunk while patrolling north of the Faroe Islands with the loss of 238 men. He was the son of William and Agnes Barrett and husband of Ellen Barrett. He is commemorated on the Memorial in the Church of St Augustine in Norwich.

Percy John William Barwick, Sergeant (Pilot) 515587, 217 Squadron, Royal Air Force, died 15 November 1939. He was the husband of D. Barwick of Walthamstow, Essex and is buried in St Mary's Churchyard, Snettisham, Norfolk.

Robert James Bottomley, Sergeant PO/22159, HMS *Royal Oak*, Royal Marines, died 14 October 1939 when his ship was sunk by torpedoes from *U-47* while at anchorage at Scapa Flow with the loss of 833 men. He was aged 36, the son of Arthur and Elizabeth Bottomley and the husband of Gladys May Bottomley. He is commemorated on Portsmouth Naval Memorial.

Burying German dead with full honours in Sheringham.

Scale model of HMS Rawalpindi.

HMS Royal Oak.

CHAPTER TWO

1940

At A Glance: Local and World events

JANUARY

Local

Bitterly cold weather hits the county with influenza and measles epidemics; rivers and harbours are frozen. Heavy shipping losses off the East Coast and the first German bombers sighted over Great Yarmouth.

World

In Britain, butter, sugar, bacon and ham are rationed.

FEBRUARY

Local

Norfolk establishes minimum wage for agricultural workers (38s per week). Convoys and armed merchant ships run along coast and down to London.

World

Some 239 British prisoners rescued from the German tanker *Altmark*. In Britain, mass evacuation of schoolchildren planned.

MARCH

Local

Ploughing campaign intensifies. Flight patrols increase out to sea off coast.

World

Peace treaty signed for Russo-Finnish conflict. In Britain, meat rationing introduced.

APRIL

Local

Coast on high alert as Germany occupies Denmark and Norway. Evacuation plans continue. As in Great War, Norfolk coastal resorts fear loss of trade.

World

Denmark and Norway attacked by Germany. In Britain, income tax increased to 7s 6d and heavier duties introduced on tobacco and alcohol.

MAY

Local

Troops posted in seaside towns as invasion fears increase; schoolchildren evacuated from coast. Norfolk bases raid Norway and Denmark. Dunkirk evacuated, using Norfolk craft. Regiments from Norfolk fight in Belgium. Local Defence Volunteers formed.

World

In Britain, aliens arrested. Norway surrenders and Germany invades Holland, Belgium, Luxembourg and France. French defeated at Sedan. Churchill forms coalition government in Britain and makes famous 'blood, toil, tears and sweat' speech. Dunkirk evacuated.

JUNE

Local

A 20-mile Coastal Belt declared. First air attacks on East Anglia and air bases.

World

Italy declares war on Britain and France. Germans enter Paris and France signs peace agreement.

JULY

Local

Battle of Britain commences in skies over Norfolk. Beaches are mined. Curfew imposed in rural districts. Norwich and Lowestoft suffer air attacks.

World

Battle of Britain begins. Hitler orders plans to be completed for invasion of Britain. French fleet attacked by Royal Navy.

AUGUST

Local

Convoys off East Coast attacked by air. Many air battles take place in Norfolk skies. Acoustic mines are laid by Germany off the East Coast. Sustained attacks take place on Norfolk RAF bases.

World

RAF bombs Berlin. United States lease-lends fifty destroyers to Britain.

SEPTEMBER

Local

Heavy onslaught continues on RAF bases. Army in East Anglia reduced from seven to four divisions. Invasion code word is issued: 'Cromwell'.

RAF Fortress B1 with 'bathtub' gondola, 1940.

World

London Blitz launched for fifty-seven consecutive nights. Hitler suspends invasion plans. Tripartite Pact is signed between Italy, Japan and Germany.

OCTOBER

Local

Heavy bombing commences over Norfolk with 289 bombs dropped in a single day. Norfolk RAF bases train for night operations. New ploughing targets are issued for farmers. Terrible 'Back of the Inns' fire breaks out in Norwich.

World

Italy invades Greece. Germans develop mixed incendiary and explosive bombs.

NOVEMBER

Local

Italy continues bombing of Norfolk towns. German flyers develop strategy of heavy machine-gunning at low altitude. Home Guard commence complete responsibility for defence duties.

World

Neville Chamberlain dies. Roosevelt is re-elected US President. First raid on Coventry kills 400.

DECEMBER

Local

With fears of invasion receding, there is some relaxation of restrictions in Coastal Defence Area. Norwich Cathedral precinct is bombed.

World

Fire blitz is increased on London and industrial cities. Hitler plans attack on Russia. Britain begins North African offensive.

The 'sinister trance'

To begin with 1940 was marked by inactivity or, as Churchill put it, a 'sinister trance'. The government was aware that people were confused: there had been massive disorganization to daily life from the evacuation of schoolchildren to blackout precautions but the enemy were not yet at the door.

Many considered restrictions excessive. It was difficult to buy torch batteries, cars were allowed only one headlight and in Norwich it was not permitted to strike a match during the blackout. Norwich installed special streetlights which gave 1/400 the illumination of those installed pre-war.

Guildhall Corner, Norwich, 1939. The building to the left was originally a Queen Anne mansion built in the early eighteenth century. There is two-way traffic being directed by a policeman.

Guildhall Corner today; the road is now a one-way street heading away from the centre.

It was also another severe winter and the officer of health in Norwich claimed that one in ten of the population had colds.

Farmers could not work at full pace due to a shortage of fuel. Rationing began on 8 January with each person being allowed twelve ounces of sugar, 4 ounces of bacon and 4 ounces of butter a week. From 11 March all meat was rationed, each adult being entitled to 1s 10d worth – enough for about 1lb of chops – and children under six were allocated half this amount. As 45 million people had registered, problems arose with ensuring that each had an equal share – besides Norfolk country folk often had access to tripe, liver, hearts, sweetbreads and rabbits, food denied their town-abiding counterparts. Blackbird shooting became all the rage among schoolboys with several recipes appearing for blackbird pies, each of which needed at least a dozen birds. Much home meat was now replaced by Argentinian and Empire frozen stocks which sold at an equivalent price. On 25 March the butter ration was doubled. Money ruled, however, as regards luxury goods. Norwich market sold pineapples, nectarines, grapes, peaches, oranges, bananas and chocolate, although the famous Caley's brand of chocolate became very rare as the Chapelfield Works – now the site of Chapelfield Shopping Centre – was forced to shed 2,000 workers.

As far as possible, entertainments continued, the most common being via the radio. Sports clubs had a bleak time as men enlisted. Theatre was very popular in Norfolk towns, although one all-girl revue, 'Meet the Girls' at the Norwich Hippodrome in February was prosecuted for being too ribald, each of the four leading actresses being fined £1. Dance Halls were packed, one of the most famous being the Samson and Hercules building in Tombland, Norwich which was to prove very popular with American airmen and even today continues partly as a commercial venue, some of it having been converted into apartments.

An independent government of East Anglia?

An embryonic Government of East Anglia was set up in Cambridge under Sir Will Spens, an ex-Vice-Chancellor of

Norwich Market 1930s.

The Market today.

Parading in Norwich city centre.

Cambridge University. Should the enemy invade and East
Anglia be cut off, then Sir Will would rule this part of Britain
exactly as he saw fit. At first, Emergency Committees were set
up but, as the 'sinister trance' continued with little evidence
of invasion, councils quickly took back their power. One vital
job for them was to distribute 35 million gasmasks. It was also
accepted by many that an extensive ARP service was needed and
recruitment from both professionals and volunteers was brisk
as people signed up to 'do their bit'. Their pay and conditions,
and the fact that they had very little to do, caused resentment.
Many considered it an outrageous waste of money when an
ARP Services Social Club boasting a billiards room, games
room, reading room and bar was opened in Norwich.

Special problems for the East Coast

Confusion reigned in holiday resorts along the East Coast. Many
still remembered the ruin of some previously successful hotels

Exercise with (almost) everyone wearing gas masks.

during the Great War and the big question as spring approached was 'Will there be any customers at all this year?' Great Yarmouth Town Council was forced to postpone a decision on

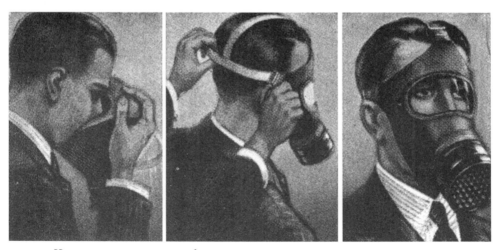

How to put on your gas mask.

whether or not to book an orchestra (it subsequently did) while Cromer was bold enough to reopen the pier which had been closed upon the outbreak of the war. Hunstanton authorized limited expenditure on advertisements for the summer holiday period. Many hoteliers and guest house owners closed off a section of their premises and reclassified these portions as warehouse accommodation in order to attract lesser rates.

A feeling grew, believed by Chamberlain and some in government, that an economic blockade might be enough to win the war and that Germany might collapse before the year was out.

The British laid down a vast minefield to try to protect shipping lanes, the mine-laying fleet sailing out from Great Yarmouth and ports to the south every day. However, the Luftwaffe, submarines and surface craft of the enemy kept up a relentless assault on merchant ships, including laying vast quantities of *their* mines. At the outset of the year, none of the

Chamberlain with the 'Munich Agreement' signed with Hitler on his return from Munich.

British merchant fleet was armed. The RAF, operating from Docking in Norfolk, arranged continuous fighter patrols.

Casualties remained high. On 8 January the motor trawler *Eta* was caught up in a mine and exploded; the next day the *Rotha* was attacked and sunk by German bombers; the Cromer lifeboat was called out to rescue thirty from the Italian steamer *Traviata* on 11 January and there were less serious attacks. The RAF managed to protect some ships, the Spitfires being particularly effective against the Heinkels.

On 29 January, the East Dudgeon lightship, manned by men from Great Yarmouth, Lowestoft and Gorleston, was attacked by a Heinkel bomber in the North Sea. In appalling ice-cold conditions, the eight-man crew managed to clamber aboard a small boat and began rowing furiously towards the shore. One man, John Sanders, succeeded in reaching the beach – the bodies of the other seven were washed up on the Lincolnshire shore. The next day SS *Royal Crown* was bombed, fifteen of her crew managing to row to shore at Southwold. It was on this date, also, that Great Yarmouth port, and the town itself, received a heavy attack.

Altogether, eleven ships were sunk along the Norfolk/ Suffolk coast during January. On 3 February an attack was made on a convoy off Cromer and on the 22nd a bombing raid failed to stop the King's Lynn ship, *Gothic*, whose captain was 70-year-old J. Cooper Nisbet, sailing on and subsequently reaching port. And so the onslaught continued until April when the Germans were distracted by other concerns.

In the air

German planes were a rarity over East Anglia during the first month of 1940 but there were occasional sorties – Great Yarmouth, for example, witnessed the enemy overhead on 30 January. There was, however, almost continual activity by the RAF which operated fifteen airfields in the region at this time with four more under construction. RAF Bomber Command was set up at Marham and Feltwell in Norfolk and Honington,

Mildenhall and Stradishall in Suffolk. Such flights as there were into enemy territory were designed primarily to drop propaganda leaflets.

Norfolk soldiers

All Norfolk's professional soldiers were serving overseas at the beginning of the year – the 1st battalion of the Royal Norfolks, for example, was in India and the 2nd Royal Norfolks were in France. Practically no information about them was available to families or the public. There was an anti-invasion plan codenamed 'Julius Caesar' which relied on large numbers of Territorial troops but, as the 'phoney war' (as some called it) continued, they had little to do and too much time on their hands. Norwich tried its best to provide entertainments, putting on a show to which 1,000 servicemen were invited, at St Andrews Hall on 30 January.

A Dornier 17 German bomber which was shot down over Norfolk and exhibited in Eaton Park, Norwich, in 1940.

Other volunteers did what they could, many groups combining to erect a building outside Thorpe station providing meals and accommodation for tens of thousands of troops in transit.

Dunkirk

'I want war. To me all means will be right…..'

Adolf Hitler

On 9 April came a change in mood as news of the German invasion of Denmark and Norway was announced – the 'phoney war' was over. It was not publicly known at the time but the British government had itself been planning an invasion of Norway. Discontent with Chamberlain grew and in early May he was replaced as Prime Minister by Winston Churchill, heading up a Coalition government.

On the same day that Churchill took up office, the Germans invaded Holland, Belgium and Luxembourg. Dutch resistance lasted five days and Belgium surrendered on 27 May. Churchill could promise 'nothing but blood, toil, tears and sweat'. There was an immediate increase in activity over Norfolk as the RAF Bomber Command began regular raids on targets between Stavanger and Aalborg.

All shipping was suspended between Harwich and the Continent at the end of April apart from two ships sent to evacuate British subjects from The Netherlands. HMS *Hereward* was also sent to bring Queen Wilhelmina and her entourage to England. There followed the Crown Princess, Dutch Ministers, diplomats, the Dutch gold reserves, the cruiser *Jacob van Heemskerck*

The new Prime Minister, Winston Churchill.

and seven submarines of the Royal Netherlands Navy. Queen Wilhelmina established the Dutch Government-in-Exile when in London and broadcast regularly on Radio Oranje.

In northern France, meanwhile, British troops were digging trenches, building roads and airfields and constructing 400 pillboxes. The British Expeditionary Force (BEF) quickly moved into Belgium and this included the 2nd Royal Norfolks. On 14 May the Germans invaded France by-passing the Maginot Line. The British cabinet began to consider a withdrawal towards Dunkirk and on 23 May all British forces facing east were withdrawn to their previous winter positions. Food was scarce and all BEF troops were placed on half rations. The Royal Norfolks were heavily involved in holding an extensive line with only two full-strength companies.

HMS Hereward.

Queen Wilhelmina talking to the Dutch people on Radio Oranje in 1940.

The Royal Norfolk's first Victoria Cross

The Royal Norfolks were to win five Victoria Crosses during the course of the war and it was for duty just after dawn of 21 May that the first was awarded to Company Sergeant Major George Gristock, aged 22. He led eight riflemen against a furious German assault on the Royal Norfolk's flank, crawled forward alone to kill a German crew of four at a gun post, was shot in both legs, made his way back and directed defence. His official citation recorded that he saved many lives by his actions. He did not live to collect his medal, however.

The British began to withdraw to a bridge-head covering Dunkirk; by 29 May the 2nd Essex Regiment and, on 29th, the Royal Norfolks, arrived on the beaches.

Company Sergeant Major George Gristock VC.

The final numbers for the evacuation from the beaches was 225,000 British officers and men, 110,000 French troops and 2,000 Belgians. The casualties were terrible, however – of the almost 1,000 men of the 2nd Royal Norfolk Battalion that had set out, only five officers and 134 men returned home safely.

All available ships along the nearby coasts had been sought out and registered in the ten days prior to the evacuation: they varied from the biggest such as the *Malines* at 2,969 tons to cabin cruisers and whelk boats. Some sank – the *Waverley* had 400 aboard when

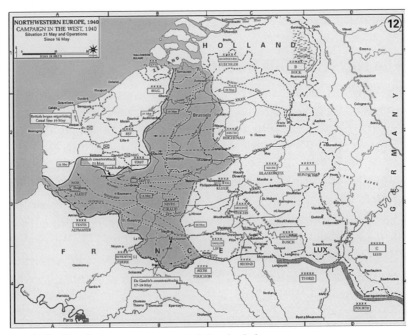

Dunkirk: The German army occupied the shaded area.

The Mona's Queen *from the Isle of Man hits a mine approaching Dunkirk.*

she was attacked and destroyed by several Heinkels – but many others carried on for three days and nights without rest and, as legend knows, came through. On railway stations transporting the troops home from the coasts a huge 'army' of volunteers assisted making tea, and distributing food – hot toast and jam was easy to make and very popular – chocolate and cigarettes.

A National Day of Prayer was declared on 27 May. On the same day Le Paradis Massacre occurred in France when ninety-seven soldiers of the Royal Norfolk Regiment were gunned down in cold blood, having run out of ammunition and surrendered to the SS under Fritz Knöchlein. At his trial for this war crime after the war he claimed several reasons for his actions, including that the Royal Norfolks had been using illegal dum-dum bullets. Following an investigation in 2015, the *Eastern Daily Press* reported that the wound inflicted by the bullets in use by the British could, on occasion, bear some relation to that caused by the notorious dum-dums. The court, however, did not believe any of Fritz Knöchlein's testimony and he was hanged in 1949.

Meanwhile life at home

In Norfolk as a whole, citizens tried to retain elements of their life as if a war was not happening. Cinemas and theatres continued to do good business and dance halls came into a life of their own. As the war progressed, the standard of film went down. There was often a feature plus a government piece such as 'Fuel Flashes', 'The Kitchen Front' or 'Battle Orders'. The few big production films were wildly popular, feeding a need for escapism and laughter. These included some still famous today: *Come on George* with George Formby, *The Murder in Thornton Square* with Charles Boyer and Ingrid Bergman, *Bulldog Drummond Strikes Again* with Ronald Colman and Loretta Young and *Goodbye, Mr Chips* with Robert Donat.

On the radio, some famous programmes were *Can you hear me, Mother?* with Sandy Powell, and *Sandy's Half-Hour* with Sandy Macpherson which, at its peak, received 5,000 requests a week for music requests from servicemen. The most famous, however, was *ITMA* (It's That Man Again) with Tommy Handley which, on Thursday evenings at 8.30 pm brought people The Minister of Aggravation and Mysteries which existed in the Office of Twerps. He invented characters such as Funf, the German spy, and Mrs Mopp, a charwoman who always entered with the ribald 'Can I do you now, Sir?'

The two most famous songs of the war were probably 'Hang out the Washing on the Siegfried Line' which sold over 200,000 copies in the first week of publication and Flannagan and Allen's 'Run Rabbit Run'.

It was on the coast that people became genuinely apprehensive, especially after the occupation of Norway and Dunkirk and, when Holland fell, enemy troops were merely 60 miles from some coastal towns. Troops were, for a time, put on duty at 10-yard intervals along the shoreline and told to be extra vigilant in their intentionally short shifts of just two hours.

St Giles Street, Norwich, 1940.

Put your gas mask on!

What seemed like an endless series of new orders was issued on everything from what to do when (if) finding a German airman hidden in a barn to the need to carry gas masks at all times (most people didn't, even after such orders). According to the BBC news, over seventy German planes had been shot down by the end of May. Exactly how the newly formed Non-Combatant Corps was to proceed in arresting anybody when they were equipped with just sticks caused much dark Norfolk humour. Spies were reported everywhere.

It was considered necessary to further move evacuated children away from the coast – many were sent to South Wales although some ignored such requests: Great Yarmouth, for instance, retained over 3,000.

Aliens were rounded up and interviewed, many of whom were Jews and vehemently opposed to Hitler. Some 500 were interned, 6,800 deemed 'uncertain' in their leanings and the rest issued with certificates of reliability. After the fall of Holland, the authorities drastically hardened their tune – sixteen Austrians and Germans were arrested in Norwich, all those classified as 'uncertain' (this was 'Category B') were arrested, including women and children, and sent to the Isle of Man and elsewhere, others being shipped to Canada.

The Emergency Powers (Defence) Act led to many more arrests including Sir Oswald Mosley and some Union activists – including three in King's Lynn – and the death penalty was extended to include almost any action deemed of assistance to the enemy. It became an offence to photograph coastal defences and cases came to court in Cromer, Norwich, Happisburgh

Bullards Brewery after the war – the site was later converted to houses and flats.

and Mundesley, heavy fines resulting for a first offence. As had happened during the Great War, some senior figures saw spies everywhere in Norfolk and the folk of this sparsely peopled county were told – by each other mainly – chilling tales of treachery, doom and spies under the bed.

Conscientious objectors were unpopular but tolerated much more than at the start of the Great War. Norwich and King's

Lynn produced a higher percentage of this group than was the case in the country as a whole. Many went into non-combatant units of the army.

The first casualty

The first casualty in Norfolk was a soldier on duty manning a searchlight near Norwich who, on Sunday, 2 June 1940 had his foot blown off by a bomb. Some descriptions of what happened after this time are necessarily vague both on security grounds and as it was now ordered that all signposts be taken down and retailers on the coast were ordered to remove all stocks of maps and guide books. Later, in late 1944, when the signposts were taken out of storage and put back, some pointed in the wrong direction for a time.

It was clear by the middle of 1940 that the country was woefully unprepared for war and Churchill knew that there

8 Section, No 4 Bomb Disposal Company, Royal Engineers remove 250kg bomb from 4, Theatre Street, Norwich in September 1940.

were not enough guns – an appeal in Norfolk produced some 2,000 firearms including some from the king's collection at Sandringham and a few ancient muskets from Norwich Museum. Nor were there enough volunteers despite Anthony Eden's plea for all able-bodied men between the ages of 17 and 65 to register. The beaches of Norfolk and Suffolk lay pretty much defenceless. Such weapons as had been collected were distributed around the towns and villages of the county, usually along with just a few rounds of ammunition.

Protection, Defence and Resistance to an invasion

Invasion was imminent – so said the Chiefs of Staff at the end of May following the appointment of General Ironside as Chief of Home Forces. The Local Defence Volunteers – soon, at Churchill's insistence, to become known as the Home Guard – were seen as vital to watch for and deal with invading airborne troops. Each Norfolk beach and port was studied and plans made for invasion contingencies. By the end of June, 786 field guns had been moved into position around the East Anglian coast. Tens of thousands of citizens of every type also helped.

In July one million First World War .303 rifles were received from the United States and immediately rushed to coastal areas where it was found that they were covered in grease – thousands of women volunteers were mobilized to clean them and within a fortnight most were useable. The Home Guard, meanwhile, was educated in the making of terrible and unstable devices known as Molotov Cocktails which could be almost any glass bottle filled with petrol, tar, oil and paraffin and which was

Lord Ironside.

to be hurled at the enemy at close range. The fledgling Home Guard were one target of William Joyce, otherwise known as Lord Haw Haw, as he took issue with them in his broadcasts which always began with 'Germany Calling. Germany Calling'. If they bore arms, he broadcast, then they would be shot as *franc-tireurs*. Although widely mocked, the broadcasts were widely listened to partly because they often contained true and accurate information about people or events. William Joyce was hanged after the war.

Also, in the whole of East Anglia it was decided to organize a secret underground resistance movement of which Andrew Croft, son of the vicar of Kelvedon in Essex, was the chief organizer. It was so secret that practically no-one ever knew of it until after the war. Major Croft was to lead a nine-man team of parachutists into German-occupied south-western France following the D-Day landings in 1944, where they were highly successful in sabotaging the retreat of German troops, in cooperation with the Maquis (rural bands of guerrilla Resistance fighters) – for three weeks they set up ambushes, blew bridges and reported back to base. Eight of the nine men survived.

On Parade.

Members of Maquis, 1944.

In 2012, a previously unknown radio bunker was discovered in Thorpe St Andrew, Norwich when the Pinebanks sports ground was being surveyed for new development. It is thought it formed one of the Zero Stations across the county for use in event of invasion. It is said to have been built under the tennis courts of the Jarrold family's home. Previously, tank traps had been discovered at Griffin Lane.

Vital, too, was the role of the seaports and naval bases, of which Harwich was by far the most important on the East Anglian coastline – seventeen ports had heavy anti-aircraft guns and many a balloon barrage. Minefields were considerably extended.

The state of the RAF

In the middle of 1940 the RAF had 700 front line fighters of which 600 were Hurricanes and Spitfires: the Germans were thought to have twice as many as well as 3,000 bombers. Airfield construction and aircraft production were prioritized. Horsham St Faiths, for example, now Norwich International Airport, had been unused for some time but was now given 264 Squadron which became the first to be equipped with the Defiant Bomber, manufactured by Boulton & Paul of Norwich.

Some airfields such as Fowlmere and Castle Camps were set up with tents instead of buildings and the remnants of squadrons that had served in France prior to Dunkirk were sent all over East Anglia. This coincided with a drive from the Luftwaffe to wipe out new bases but on the whole their raids were ineffective.

Norwich bombed

Germany also ordered increased bombings, oftentimes isolated but sometimes, such as on 19 June when Cambridge was attacked, coordinated: nine people were killed here. Then came the first raid on Norwich. On 9 July five people were killed in Sprowston in the early afternoon. At about tea time Barnards' factory in Mousehold was bombed, killing two men who were loading trucks. A bomb then exploded in Carrow Hill killing a number of workers who were pushing their bikes up the hill away from the factory gates. Boulton & Paul on Riverside suffered ten deaths as it received direct hits from four bombs, which also destroyed the railway tracks leading to the nearby Thorpe Station. Altogether twenty-seven died in this raid and several dozen were injured.

Defence Area created

On 17 June a Defence Area was created: this covered the whole of the coastal belt and included the towns of Wisbech, March, King's Lynn, Norwich, Great Yarmouth, Diss, Lowestoft, Ipswich, Stowmarket, Sudbury, Colchester, Braintree, Halstead, Chelmsford and Southend. The aim was to coordinate war work – some comparatively junior officers had been disciplined for taking on unauthorized tasks such as flooding marshes and erecting roadblocks – as well as to decide what to do in the event of invasion. Martial law was considered and rejected. Some restrictions were put in place regarding access to the beaches and coastal villages, with inevitably comic and inconsistent situations where people could not get home after a day's work or a night out as no one was quite sure what the exact rules were.

The army lobbied for a stricter regime to no effect. There was much talk about evacuating livestock in the case of an invasion but it was decided that this would be chaotic and instead all animals should be slaughtered to prevent them falling into the hands of the enemy. All small craft were to be immobilized immediately in this event and, on 28 July, a curfew was imposed from one hour after sunset to one hour before sunrise in areas deemed particularly sensitive from a military viewpoint.

Many things were banned – including 'any siren, hooter, whistle, rattle, bell, horn, gong or similar instrument'. Amateur sailors were obliged to remove their craft from coastal waterways or risk having them sunk. Kites were banned after a report in the *London Daily Sketch* of spies being caught on the Norfolk coast transmitting messages to the enemy from a kite.

There was a genuine fear at this time that an invasion was coming very soon. By the end of July about half the coastal population, around 127,000 people, had fled inland, the government lifting their liability for rent and other bills while they were away.

The Battle of Britain starts – over Norwich: Two phases

The first event of the Battle of Britain began at 4.40 in the morning of 10 July when three Spitfires from No 66 Squadron took to the air from RAF Coltishall, 8 miles north of Norwich city. They found a single German Dornier bomber which raked one of the Spitfires with bullets, forcing it back to base. The other two pursued the bomber and shot it down over the sea; three of the crew were seen adrift in the water. Soon afterwards RAF Martlesham near Ipswich was attacked by several planes and eighteen bombs dropped – fortunately any damage was limited to the edge of the airfield and there were no casualties.

There were two phases of the Battle of Britain. The first, lasting from 10 July to 12 August was designed to destroy the navy; the second, from 13 August to 15 September, to decimate the RAF. Thereupon an invasion would take place.

Luftwaffe Eagle.

For the RAF, the two chief planes for defence purposes were the Hawker Hurricane and the Spitfire. The Spitfire is perhaps more famous among the general public but it was the Hurricane that was responsible for four-fifths of all enemy aircraft destroyed – they had eight machine guns and a maximum speed of over 300 mph. The Spitfire, which was only furnished to the RAF a year before the war began, could manoeuvre beautifully making it extremely popular with pilots and was faster than the Hurricane. It was designed by Reginald J. Mitchell.

For the Germans, there was firstly the Messerschmitt 109, already tried and tested and a match for the Spitfire in most departments – it could, however, only fly for 90 minutes without refuelling. Then there was a fighter bomber, the Messerschmitt 110; the Junkers 87, the 'Stuka', the twin-engined bomber, the Junkers 88 and the two most used over Norfolk, the Heinkel 111 and the Dornier 17.

Britain had a brilliant defence system, divided into four areas. Most of Norfolk's defences were headquartered near Nottingham. The coast had searchlights at intervals of

British captured Junker 88 G-6.

Messerschmitt Bf 109 (Finnish Air Force).

6,000 yards and anti-aircraft guns. Radar had been perfected and once a plane had crossed the Channel it was monitored by the Observer Corps, one of the bases being at Norwich. As the war progressed, planes carried increasingly sophisticated radar to wipe out the German Wurzburg radars thus jamming the gunner's aim: in June 2012 the *Eastern Daily Press* reported that a receptacle containing a pristine example of one of these transmitters had been found boxed up in the cellar of a hairdressers. It is now at Muckleburgh Military Museum.

Phase 1: 10 July to 12 August

In the early morning of 11 July, three Spitfires from Coltishall sighted a lone Dornier off Great Yarmouth. It managed to escape only to shortly afterwards encounter a Hurricane piloted by the legendary Douglas Bader who was in command at Coltishall. He shot it down off the coast at Cromer. The same day Squadron Leader Peter Townsend from Martlesham was shot down in his Hurricane off Harwich by another Dornier and was rescued from the sea. German planes subsequently bombed Cromer, Yarmouth and Ipswich.

A fierce battle took place on 12 July involving planes from
Debden and Martlesham in the skies off Orford Ness when
bombers attacked a British convoy. Damage to the convoy was
minimal and two Heinkels and two Dorniers were shot down.
Two Hurricane pilots died.

Hitler ordered attacks thereafter mainly on the south
coast in anticipation of an invasion there: it was still believed,
however, that an invasion on the beaches of Norfolk and Suffolk
could occur imminently. Daily attacks continued. Norwich was
targeted on 19 and 30 July and 1 and 10 August during which
twelve people were killed.

On 1 August three Hurricanes took off from Coltishall and
shot down one of six Junkers that were bombing a convoy off
the Norfolk coast. In the next few days much shipping was lost,
including the *Cape Finisterre*, the *Drummer* and the *River Clyde*.

Heinkel He 111 bombers.

Polish pilots of 303 Squadron.

Supermarine Spitfires LF Mk 12s.

On 11 August six Hurricanes and eleven Spitfires engaged and
shot down four Messerschmitts off Harwich with two losses.
The battle recommenced some minutes later over Clacton when
one Junker and two Spitfires were shot down. RAF Martlesham
was attacked later that same day but two of the Messerschmitts
were destroyed as they headed out to sea.

On 13 August Goering launched the attack that was planned
to destroy the RAF once and for all: it failed but losses on the
south of England, not so much Norfolk, were heavy.

Women assembling Hurricanes.

A Hurricane about to be launched from a ship.

Phase 2: 13 August to 15 September

On 15 August the Luftwaffe launched five huge assaults using 1,790 planes with aerodromes a primary target. By the end of the day Germany had lost 90 planes and the RAF 42. Thereafter, day after day until mid-September, airfields were targeted by bombers with fighter support. South of London was particularly hit but Norfolk, too. Sometimes the dummy planes made at Shepperton film studios were very successful in diverting attacks from legitimate bases. In ten days 154 pilots lost their lives and 213 planes were destroyed – whilst only 65 new ones arrived from the factories.

On 19 August Honington and Coltishall were attacked and one of the returning Dorniers was shot down over Great Yarmouth. On 21 August Coltishall and Horsham St Faiths were bombed and Coltishall again two days later. Debden in Essex was attacked on 26 and 31 August. On the second occasion

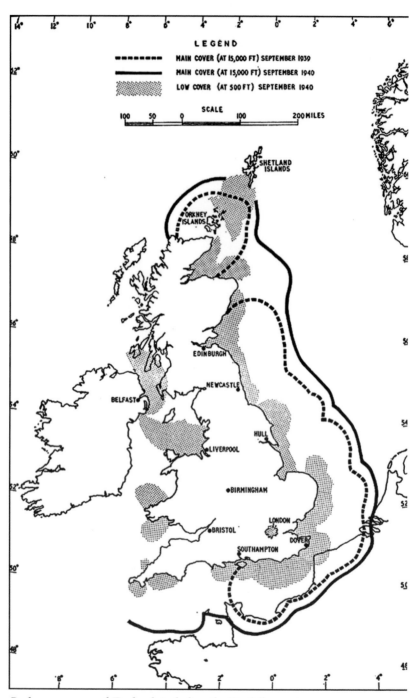

Radar cover around England, including the Norfolk coast.

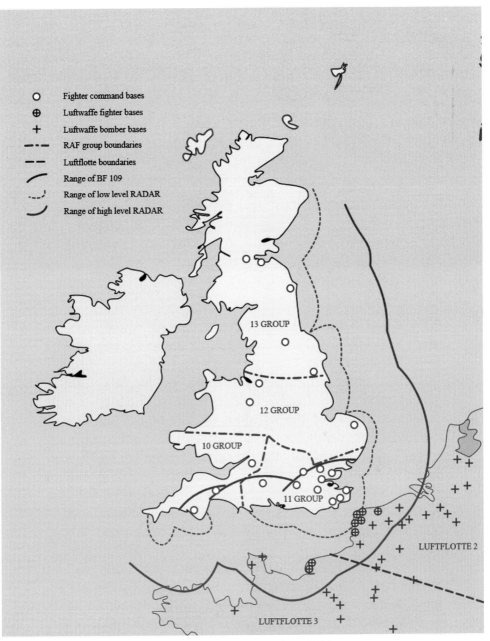

RAF and Luftwaffe bases, also showing range for Bf 109s.

Messerschmitt Me 262: there were more of these fighters during the war than any other.

200 German fighters were met by thirteen RAF squadrons from seven airfields. The skies were full of planes and it was difficult to keep track of those from both sides that crashed to earth.

Much of this fighting was south of Norfolk, around Colchester and Debden, but fighters from Norfolk's bases were scrambled. News of the ferocious attacks on the aerodromes were kept from the public as much as possible but the continual, often lone, actions of the so-called 'nuisance raids' were impossible to hide. Sometimes a street of people would be strafed, maybe a hotel or a city such as Norwich, on the 21st, selected for incendiaries. A shipyard in Cromer suffered such an attack on 23rd and on 29th Felixstowe Pier was selected. It went on and on.

The attacks on airfields reached a peak in the first week of September. Although the south took the brunt of the attacks, pilots from Norfolk were 'exchanged' with those on the south coast in order to keep up morale and offer a small respite to exhausted men. The whole of No 242 Squadron was sent from Coltishall to Duxford where they joined Nos 19 and 310 Squadrons: Douglas Bader was given command of them all and the Hurricanes operated as one 'wing' as part of the newly championed 'Big Wing' concept (basically large numbers of aircraft operated as a single formation rather than individual squadrons).

During this phase of the Battle of Britain the RAF lost 401 to Germany's 670 planes. A great build-up of barges was taking place in France for an invasion – Wellington bombers from RAF Marham in Norfolk were sent out nightly to destroy them – but, of course, the RAF had not been destroyed and so this never happened. Had the German attacks continued in the same manner for a further week it would probably have been a completely different story. But Hitler suddenly changed tack sending 348 bombers and 617 fighters to attack London on 7 September. The blitzkrieg continued for 57 consecutive nights. Goering launched a final all-out assault in the air war on 15 September when 100 Dorniers were met by 43 Hurricanes

Wellingtons under construction.

Bomb Bay of a Wellington.

from various squadrons including those commanded by Douglas Bader: the attack was completely broken. Four days later Hitler cancelled invasion plans. 'Never in the field of human conflict,' said Churchill, 'was so much owed by so many to so few.'

Some Norfolk heroes

Hubert 'Paddy' Adair flew with both 151 and 213 squadrons during the Battle of Britain. He vanished in a dogfight over

Westlegate, Norwich in 1939 and today.

Portsmouth six days after the fight effectively ended, but the place where he lost his life has never been formally identified. There is evidence recently uncovered of a crashed Hurricane and remains at Pigeon House Farm, Widley but, frustratingly, not enough evidence to identify the pilot.

George Barclay, 249 Squadron, was a Cromer vicar's son. Awarded the Distinguished Flying Cross he was shot down over France and evaded capture. He died flying over North Africa just short of his 23rd birthday. One of his successes was the shooting down on 15 September of a Dornier 17 bomber.

Thomas 'Jimmie' Elsdon, 72 Squadron, was born in Scotland and educated at Unthank College, Norwich. He secured seven victories, six of them during the Battle of Britain for which he was awarded the Distinguished Flying Cross. He ended the war in charge of RAF Boreham and was awarded the OBE. He died in 2003, aged 86.

Edward Gunter, 43 and 501 squadrons, lasted just three weeks before he was shot down over Kent and his parachute failed to open. He is buried in St Mary's Aldeby, where his father was vicar.

A Heinkel He 111 bomber over London when the raids switched from Norfolk and airfields in September 1940.

Peter Humphreys, 152 Squadron, served briefly in the Battle of Britain but earned his Distinguished Flying Cross as a fighter pilot in the Middle East. He also served in Italy. He was killed after the war in an accidental mid-air collision on Armistice Day 1947.

Arthur 'Jo' Leigh, 64 and 72 squadrons, successfully helped shoot down a Dornier 17 and three Messerschmitt 109s. He was awarded both the Distinguished Flying Medal and the Distinguished Flying Cross. After the war he settled in Norwich where he became a very successful businessman. He died in 2004.

Frederick Robertson, 66 Squadron, shared the first victory in the Battle of Britain. He had had to bale out of his Spitfire during Dunkirk when it was shot down. With a confirmed 11 victories over Malta, along with four other 'probables' he won the Distinguished Flying Medal. He was killed in 1943 in a mid-air collision over Norfolk involving an American Flying Fortress.

Frederick 'Rusty' Rushmer, 603 Squadron, was one of eleven children and is credited with the destruction of a Dornier bomber on 2 September. He subsequently failed to return from another mission over Kent and his unidentified body was buried in Staplehurst in the county. In 1990 the find of a small pocket watch at the crash site was enough to identify the body as that of 'Rusty' Rushmore and his headstone was finally engraved with his name.

Charles Stokes was not a pilot but for a time looked after the legendary Douglas Bader. His story reached a wide audience upon his death in October 2015, aged 102. He spent the last part of his life in Gaywood, King's Lynn. He was mentioned in dispatches for his engineering skill and especially for rectifying a blind spot on Hurricanes and Spitfires by utilizing mirrors on the fuselage. Prior to this the Luftwaffe had known that the aircraft were vulnerable if attacked from a certain angle. He published his autobiography at the age of 100 – it is called *Charles Stokes, A Century of Life*.

Farming, food and factories.
Gas Masks and sirens

Norfolk farmers more than adequately responded to the call from the new Minister of Agriculture, Mr R.S. Hudson, for greater efficiency. Farm prices were increased in June, as was acreage under cultivation, but some aspects of farming had to be cut back – this especially applied to pig and poultry production as feeding stuffs needed to be imported.

From July, restrictions were placed on food supplies. As in the Great War, hotels throughout Norfolk and on the coast were encouraged to offer smaller portions – it was forbidden to have both a meat and a fish course in the same meal, icing was banned and recipes for meatless stews and pies grew ever more ingenious. Tea was rationed: 2 ounces per person per week was allowed; a combination of 6 ounces of butter, margarine or cooking fat per person per week was permitted and people began making jam in maximum quantities – there were still thousands of apple trees in Norfolk at this time.

Lord Beaverbrook brought his considerable energies to factory production. As in the Great War, Boulton & Paul of Norwich was engaged in important work. During 1914–18 they had produced more of the Sopwith Camel aircraft, the type that eventually caused the demise of the legendary Red Baron, than anyone else; now they were concerned with making wooden bodies for the Oxford Trainer aircraft as well as parts for gliders. Aircraft production reached new heights. In May the RAF had only 700 frontline fighters – by July the number had increased to 496 for that one month alone while tanks – another invention that can claim to have been originally developed in Norfolk during the Great War, were being produced at a rate of 123 a month.

Metal railings were taken from churches and public buildings – many areas of Norwich such as Coslany bear the scars of this today. In the centre of town many metal railings, such as the magnificent fence and gates surrounding St Peter Mancroft, which were made by Boulton & Paul on Riverside, were spared and still survive (their name is on the gateposts).

Most people on the coast carried a gas mask – certainly not the case in Norwich where maybe one in five did. A poem doing the rounds, although humorous, gave a good idea of how a gas attack would smell:

If you get a choking feeling, and a smell of musty hay,

You can bet your bottom dollar that there's phosgene on the way.

But the smell of bleaching powder will inevitably mean

That the enemy you are meeting is the gas we call chlorine.

When your eyes begin a-twitching, and for tears you cannot see,

It isn't Mother peeling onions, but a dose of C.A.P.

If the smell resembles peardrops, then you'd better not delay,

It's not Father sucking toffee, it's that ruddy K.S.K.

If you catch a pungent odour as you're coming home to tea,

You can safely put your shirt on it, they're using B.B.C.

And lastly, while Geraniums look pleasant in a bed,

Beware their smell in War-time, if it's Lewisite your dead!

The sense of 'what will be will be' was accentuated in Norwich as during the first raid the sirens failed to go off. This then happened three more times. Ten people were killed when housing was bombed on 30 July and two days later there were further casualties after an attack on Boulton & Paul's paint shop and the machine gunning of people in the street around Thorpe station. Major firms thereafter organized their own warning systems operating from the roofs of business premises and the authorities decided not to sound any alarm for attacks by single enemy aircraft.

Inspecting gas masks, Wells 1940.

As has been remarked, the populations of coastal towns drastically reduced as people moved inland. Many businesses had no option but to shut up shop. Mass Observation sent people out to report but on some occasions encountered little more than 'ghost towns'. The town authorities could not make ends meet and some experienced severe financial problems – Great Yarmouth, for example, had to arrange a £50,000 bank loan in the early summer.

Raids during the rest of the year

After the Battle of Britain the character of the war in the air changed: less fighters diving, shrieking and weaving and more bombers, both those from the enemy going towards London and assaults launched to the Continent from East Anglian and other bases, ominously thundering overhead. The noise could be constant as night raids became a priority. This resulted in anti-aircraft gun posts coordinating with Bomber Command – Norwich received four A.A. guns at the end of August. In October a total of 289 bombs fell on Norfolk in one day, the highest of any county for a single day in the war. One new danger was the 'land mine' bomb which was dropped silently by parachute and could cause great devastation. From October the Germans also mixed incendiaries with high explosive bombs which led to a new National Fire Service being formed. From 11 November the Italians also began to launch day attacks, one being on Great Yarmouth. The Germans also tried dropping propaganda leaflets picturing a posturing Churchill as a war criminal intent on killing women and babies.

Norwich received seven more attacks after the Battle of Britain and before the year ended. The Theatre Royal had to be cordoned off when a huge delayed-action bomb was dropped in September. In October the streets in the centre were sprayed with bullets and on another occasion incendiaries were used. In December the Anglican Cathedral was slightly damaged when a bomb landed in the Cloisters. All in all, however, little damage was done on these

A soldier of the 4th Battalion, The Royal Norfolk Regiment, mans a trench at Great Yarmouth July 1940.

particular raids. By the end of the year the total number of alerts in the city had been 580 with the death toll at sixty.

In the county as a whole there were few who had not a tale to tell of seeing a falling aircraft – these could be a major hazard. This was particularly so sometimes in the coastal areas as retreating planes swooped in low in order to drop any remaining bombs and were consequently more vulnerable to gunfire from increasingly well-equipped defences. For example, Great Yarmouth had four 6-inch and two 12-pounder guns by this time. It was also helpful that the Home Guard was considered well trained and equipped enough to take the brunt of coastal defence duties which in turn released regular soldiers for other tasks.

Hitler's secret airfields?

There is a story in Norfolk, some dismissing it as complete nonsense, that Hitler was planning secret airfields in the area.

The claim is that it was only in 1940 that these were finally spotted by the RAF, scouting for airfields of its own. The airstrips were on 2,000 acres of farmland and had been built from 1936 by a nest of enemy spies who were secretly working for the Third Reich. One landing spot comprised two farms at Sporle, near King's Lynn, 16 miles from Sandringham. Another 'hidden aerodrome' was 25 miles away at Guestwick. It is claimed that each airstrip, with hangars disguised as outbuildings, covered at least 200 acres. Every barn had a red roof to help pilots. According to this theory, the undercover operatives built nine airfields in Norfolk and one near Woking, in Surrey. They lived among the families of Norfolk.

Some Norfolk Soldiers, Sailors and Airmen

Vera Adeline Batley, Civilian War Dead, died in the General Hospital, Great Yarmouth, 11 July 1940, having been injured at 25 Gordon Road.

Robert John Bird, Chief Steward, H.M. Yacht *Sappho*, Naval Auxiliary Personnel (M.N.) died on 29 September 1940, aged 35. He was the son of Martha Bird of Holt, Norfolk. He has no known grave and is commemorated on Liverpool Naval Memorial.

Mr Arthur Cyril Bracey, Civilian, was one of nine employees of Boulton & Paul's Engineering Works near Thorpe Station

Mk I Hurricane in France, 1939.

who were killed on 1 August 1940 by two bombs dropped by a Junkers 88. He was 24, the son of A.A. and E.F. Bracey of 25 Leonard Street, Norwich, Norfolk. He was the husband of D.E. Bracey of 9 Caston Road, Thorpe, Norwich, Norfolk. He is buried in Norwich Cemetery and commemorated on the Memorial in St Augustine's Church, Norwich.

Basil Mark Fisher, Flying Officer (Pilot) 72382, 111 Squadron, Royal Air Force, died 15 August 1940. He had attended Eton and Trinity College, Cambridge where he read Modern Languages and History before joining the RAF and becoming operational in May 1940. His Hurricane P3944 was shot down in flames over Selsey and, although managing to bale out, he did not survive. He was the son of George and Janet Fisher. He is buried in Eton (St John) Church Cemetery, Buckinghamshire. His brother, Flying Officer A. Fisher, also

HMS Glorious.

served in 111 Squadron and survived the war. His father, Captain George Kenneth Fisher, eldest son of George Fisher, Bishop of Southampton and Honorary Canon of Norwich, was killed in action whilst on patrol in Egypt on 3 September 1917.

Stanley Goodrum, Driver, 9 Troop Carrying Company, Royal Army Service Corps, died on Sunday 2 June 1940 during the evacuation of Dunkirk, aged 20. He is commemorated on the Dunkirk Memorial.

Edward Maurice Gunter, Pilot Officer (Pilot) 83988, 501 Squadron, Royal Air Force Volunteer reserve, died on 27 September, aged 20, when his parachute failed to open following a skirmish between his Hurricane 1 V6645 and the enemy over Sittingbourne, Kent. He was the son of William and Margery Gunter of Aldeby and he is buried in the churchyard of St Mary, Aldeby, Norfolk.

Stanley Holman, Able Seaman C/SSX 15731, HMS *Mendip*, Royal Navy, died 24 October 1940 aged 23. He was the son of Frank and Priscilla Holman and husband of Florence Esther Holman. He has no known grave and is commemorated on Chatham Naval Memorial.

Robert Mark Livermore, Sergeant 550254, 101 Squadron, Royal Air Force, died on 5 July 1940, aged 21. He was the son of Thomas and Mary Ann Livermore of Mundesley-on-Sea, Norfolk. He is commemorated on Runnymede Memorial, Surrey, Panel 16.

Trevor Patrick Smith, Air Fitter, FAA/FX 75623, Royal Navy was killed on HMS *Glorious* on 8 June 1940 when, together with HMS *Acasta* and HMS *Ardent*, she was sunk in the Norwegian sea by German battlecruisers *Gneisenau* and *Scharnhorst* with the total loss of 1,500 men. He was aged 20 and the son of William and Gladys Smith of Great Yarmouth. He has no known grave and is commemorated on the Memorial at Lee-on-Solent.

Spencer Malcolm Welch, Able Seaman C/J 109700, HMS *Whirlwind*, Royal Navy, died at sea 5 July 1940. The ship was torpedoed by submarine *U-34* west of Land's End, England. Spencer Welch has no known grave and is commemorated on Chatham Naval Memorial.

Albert Walter Winn, Private 5774182, 7th Battalion Royal Norfolk Regiment, died on 12 June 1940, aged 35. He was the son of Timothy and Ann Winn and husband of Florence M. Winn of Hunstanton, Norfolk. He is commemorated on Dunkirk Memorial, France, Column 44.

CHAPTER THREE

1941

At A Glance: Local and World events

JANUARY

Local

The weather is bitterly cold. New evacuation of schoolchildren from London to eastern counties begins. Luftwaffe launches continuous attacks on East Coast shipping. Some East Anglian battalions are posted to Scotland as part of 18th Division.

World

Germany attempts to blockade UK. Italians retreat in North Africa. Joint talks in secret between Britain and the US about possible American involvement in war.

FEBRUARY

Local

Norfolk farmers exceed ploughing quotas. Air raids take place on Norwich and East Coast ports. Towns and villages organize groups to fight fires.

World

Some 130,000 are taken prisoner as Italians routed in North Africa. Rommel arrives in Tripoli. British troops fight in Greece. Malta is attacked. Germany has success in sinking Atlantic shipping.

MARCH

Local

Some 145 raid alerts are issued at Norwich. Invasion committees formed. More evacuees arrive from London.

World

Lend-Lease bill is passed in US. British commandoes launch successful operation on Lofoten Islands. British troops increased in North Africa and Greece. Allies see Abyssinian advance.

APRIL

Local

Extensive damage suffered in raids against Great Yarmouth and Norwich factories. Gas warfare is feared.

World

London and Plymouth are bombed. RAF bombs Kiel and Wilhelmshaven. Germans advance in North Africa. Greece and Yugoslavia surrender.

Arrival of evacuees.

MAY

Local

East Anglia holds major anti-invasion exercise involving 75,000 troops. East Coast convoys continue to undergo heavy losses.

World

Hess flies to Scotland on peace mission and is imprisoned. The Allies evacuate Greece. *Bismarck* sunk.

JUNE

Local

King's Lynn bombed.

World

Germany invaded Russia. Rommel successfully defends Tobruk.

JULY

Local

Some 170,000 troops and civil defence forces hold anti-invasion exercise. Shortage of some foodstuffs including eggs and cheese. Some pubs run out of beer.

World

Germany makes rapid advances into Russia.

AUGUST

Local

Norwich holds 'stay-at-home' Bank Holiday and 20,000 flock to Eaton Park. New minimum wage of 54 shillings per week for farm workers is introduced.

World

Churchill and Roosevelt sign Atlantic Charter. Royal Navy relieves Tobruk.

SEPTEMBER

Local

New airfields are built. People are encouraged to forage for wild food such as blackberries.

World

Kiev falls and Leningrad is isolated. Losses are great from U-boat attacks.

OCTOBER

Local

Largest ever exercise undertaken to simulate an invasion of East Anglia.

World

RAF raids Hamburg and Bremen. Soviet government moves from Moscow to Kuibyshev.

NOVEMBER

Local

Farm workers are awarded new minimum wage of £3 per week.

World

German advance is halted in Russia as the weather deteriorates. Allied offensive is launched in Libya. The *Ark Royal* is sunk.

DECEMBER

Local

Norfolk holds many 'Aid to Russia' parties.

World

Japanese bomb Pearl Harbor. HMS *Repulse* and HMS *Prince of Wales* are sunk with great loss of life. US declares war. Tobruk is relieved.

Standing alone

At the beginning of 1941 Britain stood alone, the propaganda myth of 'victory' at Dunkirk and the heroics of the Battle of Britain notwithstanding. Norway, The Netherlands, Denmark, France and Belgium had been taken. Troops were billeted in practically every town and village of Norfolk, which gave some reassurance to the general public who did not know of the severe shortages of ammunition and guns. Churchill realized that victory would come only with the involvement of the United States.

Life on the Norfolk coast was especially frantic as the Germans continually laid mines which were swept daily by the coastal trawlers and drifters in order to allow vital convoys through. The RAF, flying Hurricanes from Martlesham Heath – where they were led by Douglas Bader – and Coltishall, did their best to keep the skies clear of the Luftwaffe.

Rationing was extended to a miscellaneous collection of foodstuffs – ox cheek, syrup, hearts and sweetbreads among many others which depended on where you lived. A blackout was imposed after dark and there were many accidents, particularly as batteries for cyclists' and car drivers' lights were difficult to come by. To add insult to injury, the snow came down in drifts of up to 5 feet in some places, including Great Yarmouth.

Bombing raids during the first half of the year

The people of Norfolk were already used to bombs but the scale of the raids increased and the bombs themselves were becoming ever more deadly – very few before 1941 had been more than 250 kilograms but as the year progressed some were ten times that amount. Destruction of private property was massive but industry kept on going. In Norwich some firms, including Boulton & Paul and Laurence Scott & Electromotors Ltd, cooperated in setting up a steel pylon tower high up at 15 Bracondale to spot enemy aircraft – it was by many accounts a freezing job being on duty.

The NAAFI Club, Norwich, was very well appointed and housed on a site subsequently taken over by Marks & Spencer in the early 1950s.

Raids on the county's capital city were continuous. A largely ineffective raid on 5 January was followed by a much more destructive one on a dark night, 4 February. Boulton & Paul's joinery shop was hit and three houses destroyed – two people were killed.

Vauxhall Street and Walpole Street were bombed on 18 February. The Vauxhall Tavern was destroyed and fifty houses damaged to the extent that they had to be evacuated. Neighbours gathered around to offer blankets, food and tea. Barnards Ltd was bombed and the premises machine gunned on 27 February but no lives were lost nor was production interrupted. Tombland – nothing to do with tombs but deriving from the Norse word for 'empty space' – suffered incendiaries on further raids on 14 and 15 and also at the end of March. In March altogether there were 145 warnings which lasted on average for just over an hour each.

More serious was an attack by a Dornier in daylight on 2 April – it dropped two H.E. bombs on Boulton & Paul and

*Blacking-out the windows with custom-
made curtains; many people used black
cloth and sticky tape.*

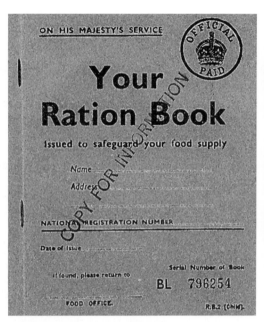

Thorpe Station resulting
in one person being killed.
Further bombings at the
end of April targeted the
city's industrial area –
Boulton & Paul again and
Reckitt & Colman's at
Carrow Road when it took
five hours to bring the fires
under control. One man
and an elderly woman were
killed.

Great Yarmouth Market, about 1940.

On 6 and 7 May the affluent areas of Unthank Road and Earlham were bombed, in the latter 150 people being made homeless and five members of one family of eight being killed.

On the Norfolk coast, Great Yarmouth along with its southern neighbour, Lowestoft, suffered almost continuous harassment. Over half the population of this coastal belt had been evacuated and this saved countless lives. The raid on Yarmouth and nearby Gorleston on 7–8 April destroyed more property than any other in the war over the whole of East Anglia. Mines drifting down on parachutes as well as incendiary and H.E. bombs caused devastation and also fractured some

A similar view of the market today.

Dealing with a gas fracture alongside Norwich City Hall.

water mains which further hampered rescue work. Roads were rendered impassable. Many of the major stores were ruined including Marks & Spencer, Rise's Fashions and Boots the Chemist. Seventeen people died during the night. The Luftwaffe came again in the morning with H.E. and incendiary bombs and further damaged the towns' industrial premises. It has later been estimated that 4,000 incendiary bombs had by this time been dropped on Yarmouth and Gorleston. In early June there were more raids on Yarmouth, killing twelve people.

The Duke of Kent visited on 25 April.

In March, May and June, King's Lynn was also attacked, Whitefriars Terrace being one of the streets damaged in the June raid during which sixteen people died. Many people were now equipped, free of charge, with the new 'Morrison' shelter which resembled a metal table into which two adults and two children could crawl. As the local press had reported during the Great War, the curiosity of the public knew no bounds as crowds rushed to each scene of destruction. Looting, however, was almost non-existent as court records verify.

Out at Sea; Henry Blogg and the Lifeboats

The Germans continued to inflict losses through mines and attacks on convoys. 'Pocket battleships', especially the *Admiral Scheer* and *Admiral Hipper*, were deadly: by 1 April the former had sunk seventeen Allied vessels and the latter, at the end of February, destroyed seven out of nine ships in one unescorted convoy.

In May came the most crucial battle yet. Having spotted the battleship *Bismarck* and the heavy cruiser *Prinz Eugen*, the Naval Command sent the cruiser *Hood* and the battleship

Boulton & Paul Defiant. Boulton & Paul were originally a Norwich company, beginning in the city in 1797. They produced more of the famous Sopwith Camel aircraft during the Great War than anyone else. From 1936 the aircraft business was based in Wolverhampton.

Prince of Wales to join up with the British Fleet. On 24 May a shell from the *Bismarck* exploded a magazine in the *Hood* which sank within three minutes: 1,416 men were lost and only three survived. The *Bismarck* was attacked by the *Prince of Wales* and a torpedo from a plane on the aircraft carrier *Illustrious*. She did not sink. Finally after being shelled by *King George V* and *Renown* a torpedo from the cruiser *Dorsetshire* sent the pride and joy of the German navy to the bottom: 2,100 men were killed.

Less spectacular damage was occurring in the North Sea with the loss of one vessel every two days on average. Sometimes collisions in the pitch black of night sank some of the navy's finest craft – the brand new submarine HMS *Umpire*, for example, was struck by a trawler with the loss of twenty-two men.

Henry Blogg, a hero of the Great War, continued his exploits in the second. He was now 65 years of age. He was three times awarded the Gold Medal of the RNLI.

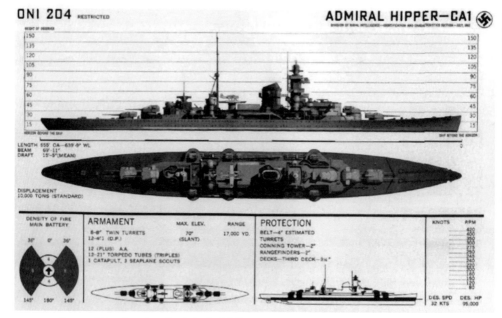

Recognition drawing for Admiral Hipper.

On 6 August six merchantmen grounded off Haisborough Sands, north-east of Cromer. At 8 am Blogg skippered the *H.F. Bailey* to the *Oxshott* where he found sixteen men roped together and, in a desperately dangerous rescue from an unstable vessel in stormy seas, took all the men aboard. He then took the thirty-one crew of the *Gallois* to safety. The *H.F. Bailey* was now joined by the number 2 Cromer lifeboat and the *Louise Stephens* of Gorleston which rescued thirty-one more men from the other ships. Blogg then went to the aid of the *Deerwood* where nineteen crewmen were taken aboard and then onto the *Paddy Hendly* saving twenty-two. The forty-one men were being taken to Great Yarmouth when hailed by a destroyer which took them aboard leaving Blogg to investigate a minesweeping trawler from which his crew took two bodies. He reached Yarmouth nine hours after setting out from Cromer.

Henry Blogg was awarded the third clasp to his RNLI Gold Medal and the British Empire Medal. For this one day alone other Norfolk lifeboat crew received a total of seven medals and

Survivors from the Bismarck *being pulled aboard HMS* Derbyshire.

eighteen vellum citations together with £117 in cash between them.

Lifeboats from other Norfolk stations were continually active. They were, for instance, called to rescue airmen from downed planes. In the autumn, the Sheringham lifeboat took aboard five Polish airmen from a Wellington bomber – they had spent seventeen hours drifting in a rubber dinghy. The Wells lifeboat also took in six airmen, again from a crashed Wellington.

HMS Hood.

HMS Hood's *15-inch Mk 1 guns.*

The last sighting of the Hood *from the* Prince of Wales.

Decoy sites, blackouts and exercises

Decoy sites were one aspect of defence against air attacks. Some industrial plants and railway stations were provided with 'dummies'. One of the most remarkable of these was the decoy site for Colchester railway station which was built just outside the town and had men pulling ropes with lights on, up and down imaginary tracks in the night time. The main RAF stations in East Anglia were also given decoy sites and these were: Bircham Newton, Duxford, Feltwell, Honnington, Marham, Martlesham, Mildenhall, Wattisham, Watton and West Raynham.

Blackouts for civilians were rigidly imposed, one result of which was that people could not see where they were going and fatal accidents increased by 40 per cent in the first two years of

Memorial to Henry Blogg on the cliffs at Cromer.

the war – reckless driving of army vehicles being one cause. As in the Great War, there were reports of people, unaware of exactly where they were, entering someone else's house and of much injury caused by umbrella tips in the dead of night. Everyone was supposed to carry an identity card in case they got lost but many did not.

The threat of invasion was ever-present, although the exclusion area around the Norfolk coast was decreased from 20 miles inland to 5. Late April 1941 saw a major invasion exercise involving 75,000 troops undertaken. This

Weybourne to Sheringham. (Daniel Tink)

Troops march through Tombland, Norwich.

was followed in June by an even bigger one involving 170,000 regular troops, 20,000 Home Guards and all of the civil defence services. There was simultaneously recruitment of many

Night exercises on the Norfolk coast.

Road blocks and exercises in Overstrand Road, Cromer.

thousands for the 'Auxiliary Field Units', i.e. the resistance movement following a successful enemy invasion.

By this time it was required that all men between the ages of nineteen and forty-one report for service in the armed forces.

Evacuees

By winter 1941 over 1.3 million people had been moved – all the Norfolk coastal towns had seen their population cut in half or more. The councils faced bankruptcy as rates could not be collected from shops and businesses that had closed down. In addition, people were arriving in the inland communities from London: many locations were faced with a 'pincer' movement with strangers coming from two directions.

One evacuee who spent, according to his memoirs, several very happy years at North Runcton was Sir Michael Caine who arrived to escape the Blitz, with his mother, Ellen, and brother, Stanley at the age of 7. He apparently made his stage debut at the village school when he was 10. In 2016 the house in which he lived was offered for sale at £400,000.

On the whole, evacuation went well at first: people wanted to help and more than sixty evacuees' social

Poster: how to spot a German soldier.

clubs were set up in Norfolk. There were problems, however, especially where people from the crowded suburbs of London arrived in an isolated Norfolk village – one boy of 15 from Islington hanged himself. Stories began to circulate that London evacuees brought fleas and ticks and many local people refused to let them into the house with the result that some compulsory billeting orders were issued. Some evacuated families simply returned to the city. There are stories of every kind in the private diaries of the period, from evacuees being taken in by kind and rich people who offered them dream beds and meals, to tales of wicked witches – some children actually believed that they had been billeted with them – who starved their charges and stole any food parcels that were sent by family members. Parents often could not afford to pay the 'required' rate of 2 shillings a week for each child: the billetors received 10/6d for the first child and 8s/6d for each subsequent one. For a mother and child together, the billetor received, weekly, 5s per adult and 3s per child – the mother was required to buy all food and cook it in the home. Sometimes there were two mothers sharing the same kitchen and this may or may not have worked.

A further problem was that some on the Norfolk coast would not budge. A Mass Observation representative reported that this was a particular problem in Great Yarmouth.

The Dominions offered an alternative home, although Winston Churchill was against the idea. Norwich sent sixty-two children to Canada in 1942 and it was reported in the local press later in the year that they were living off the fat of the land and gaining weight, something not likely to endear the scheme to the long-suffering locals.

Food and farms

Inevitably, there was a shortage of men in the right places on farms to do the necessary work. On 19 April all women aged twenty-one were required to register under a Registration for Employment Order. At first, Norfolk farmers were less than wholeheartedly enthusiastic at the prospect of allowing women to work on their land. The 'Land Girls', however, quickly became highly efficient at almost every farm task. Child labour was reintroduced and schoolboys also helped out – the senior pupils at King Edward VII in King's Lynn, for example, were released for some days to pick peas. Permanent summer time was adopted to maximize the working day.

Government decided that as much land as possible should be brought under cultivation. This was especially troublesome in some areas of Norfolk – for instance, 520 acres designated for crops in Acle – between Norwich and Great Yarmouth – tended to flood and there were similar problems in marshland near King's Lynn and in the saltings between Wells and Holkham.

Norfolk was given target production figures – to plant 3,500 acres of peas and a further 3,000 acres of potatoes and 700 acres of onions. In return farmers were given guaranteed prices for

First evacuees reach Fakenham, September 1939.

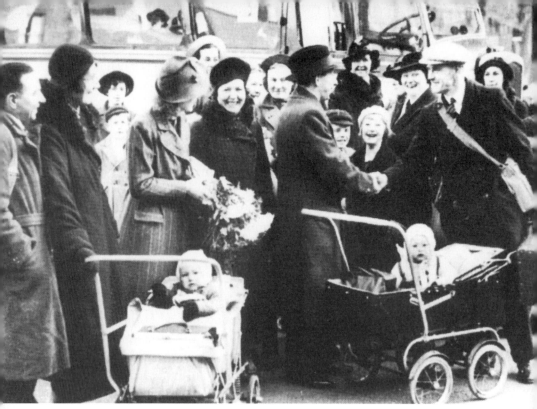

Greeting the newcomers.

these crops. Livestock was not a prominent feature of Norfolk farming at this time.

Every village was allocated a 'food production advisor' and the aim was to make each community self-sufficient in vegetables and, to a lesser extent, fruit.

By the end of the year, Norfolk had excelled in its allotted tasks: for example, it had grown about a quarter of Britain's sugar beet crop, over a third of the blackcurrants and had brought 750,000 acres under cultivation.

Everyone had to have a ration card as meat, sugar and butter were restricted. In February a 'national wholemeal loaf' was introduced made of 85 per cent extraction flour and, in most places in Norfolk, white bread was not available. Eggs, tobacco and sugar were in meagre supply and people would go on expeditions to find oranges and lemons – news of a shipment of citrus fruits from, say, South Africa to Yarmouth, quickly spread and once the bulk had been distributed to hospitals and the various services, a keen auction would take place for

Women harvesting beetroot.

Queen Elizabeth talks to a Land Army girl on a visit to Sandringham Estate.

the remainder, maximum price allowed 6½ pence a pound. Profiteers were despised and heavily fined if caught.

In December tinned meats, fish and vegetables were brought under a points rationing system and the Ministry of Food encouraged the setting up of Kitchen Clubs to give demonstrations of efficient cooking. Some people still wasted food and were brought to court.

British Restaurants

Winston Churchill championed the setting up of 'communal feeding centres' although he hated that term as it reminded him of communism and the workhouse. Thus they became 'British Restaurants' and fantastically popular they were, too. For, say, lunch you bought a token, from 1 penny to 6: 1d (old term for a penny) would buy a bowl of soup and a piece of bread while 6d bought a substantial three course meal. Diss restaurant produced 2,427 meals in the first fortnight. Swaffham, Great Yarmouth, Dereham (50,846 dinners in the first year) and Norwich followed. The British Restaurant in Norwich was at the Bull Close School and also offered dancing afterwards. There was usually a paid cook and maybe one paid helper but all other work was voluntary.

Schools were also encouraged to cook hot midday meals for the children. For some reason, Norfolk lagged behind the rest of the country in this.

Petrol was also rationed – the more powerful the car the larger the ration. All, of course, was imported and the Norwich courts dealt harshly with those who 'fiddled' their allowance. Some magistrates and other noted citizens reverted to a pony and trap to set an example.

One sad result was that cats and dogs were increasingly abandoned, the latter sometimes 'attaching' themselves to an army camp or a canteen. They could also be a menace to in-lamb flocks in the countryside. In one year alone, 200,000 dogs were destroyed. Alternatively, a dog could spend the war in Ireland or elsewhere for 10 shillings a week in kennel fees.

A British Restaurant.

A critical series of changes

'A soldier will fight long and hard for a piece of coloured ribbon.'

Napoleon

A view of Castle Hill c1941.

On 22 June, Germany invaded Soviet Russia and the main weight of Hitler's attacks swung to the east. Meanwhile, Britain had been engaging with Roosevelt in vital ways, including organizing the visits of American top brass to East Anglia where they approved construction of new air bases, even though it was not until the Japanese attack on Pearl Harbor on 7 December that Britain and America formally became full allies.

Dozens of airfields were under construction in Norfolk, each costing as much as a million pounds: hedgerows, trees and land needed to be cleared, tens of miles of roads, drains and water courses built, accommodation of all sorts put up and runways, each of which needed 175,000 cubic yards of concrete, laid down.

In March 1941 Churchill and Roosevelt signed the Lend-Lease Bill and on 12 August put their signatures to the Atlantic Charter.

'I say that the supply of needed supplies to Britain is imperative. I say that this can be done; it must be done; and it will be done…..'

President Franklin D. Roosevelt, 27 May 1941

A bizarre event happened in May when Rudolf Hess flew himself to Scotland apparently to discuss peace: he was captured and interned.

Entertainment at home

There was much discussion about the morality of enjoying yourself. There was a week of prayer in January and discussion about pub opening hours as well as whether cinemas should open on Sundays (OK, said the magistrates at King's Lynn, provided the entertainment was of a 'healthy nature'). Some cinemas also donated a percentage of their Sunday takings to hospital funds. Apart from the pub and cinema, the main mass entertainment was the radio – embryonic television transmission had been suspended at the beginning of the war. Soon the Americans would come and, with them, dances, including those at the famous Samson and Hercules building in Norwich, but this was not yet.

Sheringham just prior to the outbreak of war.

Football, horse-racing, theatrical shows and art exhibitions continued. The Maddermarket Theatre in Norwich faced closure for a while but managed to relaunch its fortunes with an Irish comedy *Spring Meeting* in September. Diana Churchill, the Prime Minister's daughter starred in an April production of *On Approval* at the Theatre Royal. Both theatres continue today, the Maddermarket using amateur actors and the Theatre Royal, professionals.

During the Great War, the local press had run some humorous articles on the reading habits of the Norfolk population – apparently, as people were forced to stay indoors they began to embrace 'greater literature', presumably the classics. So, too, during this war, books taken out from Norfolk libraries reached

Sheringham High Street today.

record levels with some citizens complaining that libraries were closed during air raids.

People obviously also had to holiday at home. Sometimes this meant that they illegally entered the defence area and the courts had to deal with several hundred cases during 1941 – a moderate fine was the usual punishment. Norwich and other areas tried to put on special entertainments, for example 20,000 attended a gala party in Eaton Park in the summer.

Cases of bigamy increased as husbands and wives were forced apart for long periods and the court records show regular prosecutions. Juvenile delinquency increased to the extent that institutions for young offenders were full.

A new phase of the war opens

High Flight

Oh! I have slipped the surly bonds of Earth
And danced the skies on laughter-silvered wings;
Sunward I've climbed, and joined the tumbling mirth
Of sun-split clouds - and done a hundred things
You have not dreamed of - wheeled and soared and swung
High in the sunlit silence. Hov'ring there.
I've chased the shouting wind along, and flung
My eager craft through footless halls of air.
Up, up the long delirious burning blue
I've topped the wind-swept heights with easy grace
Where never lark, or even eagle flew.
And while with silent lifting mind I've trod
The high untrespassed sanctity of space,
Put out my hand and touched the face of God.

John Magee
9 June 1922–11 December 1941

Like Rupert Brooke, whom he admired, John Magee had been educated at Rugby. He died in a mid-air collision over Lincolnshire where he is buried.

The RAF had been busy in a regular, sustained series of raids throughout 1941, since the first from Martlesham in January in which Hurricanes and a dozen Blenheim bombers attacked Pas de Calais. Usually these raids, which became routine by the summer, consisted of four Lancaster or Halifax heavy bombers or a squadron of Blenheims accompanied by up to thirty-six Spitfires. It is now the stuff of legend, and film, that on one of these raids Wing Commander Douglas Bader collided with a Messerschmitt bf 109 and lost his artificial legs, a new pair of which were parachuted to him at the German-occupied airfield at St Omer-Longuenesse. They were sent from RAF Horsham St Faiths in Norwich.

In August 2014, when he died, the *Eastern Daily Press* told the story of one man who was shot down in his Blenheim in 1941 – Sergeant Reginald Drake from Norwich, who spent the next three years in the notorious Stalag Luft III camp. In 1944 he took part in a forced march from Lithuania to Poland.

Another man taking part in the raids on Cologne in mid-August was Squadron Leader Bill Edrich in his Blenheim. He was awarded the DFC for his part in the raids. He was a Norwich schoolboy born in Lingwood and subsequently one of the greatest batsmen who ever played cricket for England. In 1947 he scored 3,539 runs and took 67 wickets in the season, only overshadowed on the batting score by one, Denis Compton, who made 3,816. He was also famous for never flinching in the face of a pace attack, his body, on one or two occasions, becoming badly bruised.

By September the war entered a new phase with Churchill calling for the formation of an Expeditionary Force. By this

John Gillespie Magee.

RAF Martlesham Heath, 1946.

time Germany occupied virtually the whole of Europe and had a heavy presence in the Mediterranean and North Africa. Singapore sought urgent reinforcements but Churchill refused to weaken the Middle East strength.

At this time all men between the ages of eighteen and sixty were required to register for Civil Defence duties and were liable for 48 hours' duty a month. Youngsters between sixteen and eighteen were encouraged to join the Air Training Corps – four squadrons were formed in Norwich.

Women were encouraged to work in a whole range of jobs previously done by men – in forestry, factories and on the

Douglas Bader by Cuthbert Orde.

buses and trains. Not everyone thought this was a good idea. In the Great War some had thought that it would somehow 'coarsen' a woman's finer qualities if they took up such jobs: now, one cry was 'and who will look after all the babies?'

Iron railings were removed for munitions and in Norwich some parts of the city fared worse than others. This was not the first phase of this operation and, on the whole, the city centre escaped the metal collectors although one letter in the local press could see absolutely no reason why the art-deco lions

Colditz Castle, where Douglas Bader spent almost three years.

This Bf 109 fighter, is severely damaged but managed to return to base.

outside the City Hall should not contribute to the national need – they were designed by Alfred Hardiman and had been ordered from the British Empire Exhibition of 1936. Similarly some believed the metal doors featuring eighteen plaques by James Woodward commemorating the main trades of the city – including shoe, beer, chocolate and mustard production were ugly and should be put to good war use. Both the lions and the doors are still there.

Almost everything that could be recycled was collected – foil, paper, rags, bones and even binoculars. The government also tried to take money out of circulation, principally by encouraging people with the slogan 'Don't Spend – Lend.' Special savings weeks raised huge sums of money – In East Anglia Cambridge was the star, managing to produce £4,000,000 in eighteen months. The small village of Sustead, near Cromer, raised £6,202 from only 110 inhabitants.

Soon, people all over Norfolk witnessed the results of their money-raising labours as fighting vehicles of every type were to be seen in almost all villages.

The government increasingly requisitioned buildings for war use and one of these was the Cliftonville Hotel on the Cromer cliffs.

The Cliftonville Hotel as it is today.

Norfolk nurses.

*Shoring up the New City Hall
with sandbags.*

The situation at the year's end

The last three months of the year saw some of the most dramatic episodes: Germany besieged Leningrad; Japan bombed Pearl Harbor and began invasions of countries and territories in the Far East; the United States declared war on Germany, Italy and Japan; and Rommel was challenged by a major offensive in North Africa.

'When I said that British fighter-bombers had shot up my tanks with 40mm shells, the Reichsmarschall who felt himself touched by this, said: "That's completely impossible. The Americans only know how to make razor blades." I replied: 'We could do with some of those razor blades, Herr Reichsmarschall.'

Field Marshal Erwin Rommel

Russia suddenly became a key ally of Britain and the Deputy Prime Minister, Clement Attlee, claimed during a visit to Norwich in October that 'Russia's struggle is our struggle.' The two main theatres in the city put on shows highlighting Russian traditions and culture and Anglo-Soviet Friendship Committees were formed all over Norfolk.

'In Hitler's launching of the Nazi campaign on Russia, we can already see, after six months of fighting, that he has made one of the outstanding blunders in history.'

Winston Churchill to the House of Commons,
11 December 1941

Some 15,000 men from East Anglia, including those from the Royal Norfolk Regiment, sailed to war in October, to Nova Scotia, then Cape Town and on to Mombasa and Bombay, although their families had no idea at the time where they were. Soon most of these men would be prisoners of the Japanese.

Norfolk had suffered during the year. Norwich had had 673 alerts and 969 'crash warnings'; 21 people had been killed and 104 injured. Great Yarmouth had fared worse: 109 had been killed and 329 injured; almost 10,000 houses and almost 1,000 other buildings had been destroyed or badly damaged.

It is claimed that the British sense of humour helped and continued undimmed – witness one story that a baby born at Peterborough station was called Eleanor (the railway company was L.N.E.R. – London and North Eastern Railway Company).

Life in Norfolk was grim in all sorts of ways but there was now a feeling that this was a war that could – eventually – be won.

Some Norfolk Soldiers, Sailors, Airmen and Civilian Dead

Harold Barlow, Ordinary Seaman P/JX 243001, HMS *Prince of Wales*, died on 24 May 1941 when his ship sustained damage during HMS *Hood*'s attack on the *Bismarck*. He was

One of the pair of lions guarding the 'new' City Hall.

10 Points about the Scrap Iron Campaign

1. In the whole output of steel in this country, 65 per cent of the raw material used is scrap iron and steel.

2. Every ton of scrap salvaged at home saves the importation of a ton from overseas.

3. There are thousands of tons of scrap iron and steel rusting away in the fields, farms, and cottages of England and Wales.

4. The Iron and Steel Control, Ministry of Supply, Caxton House East, Tothill Street, London, S.W.1, is now organizing the collection of this iron and steel scrap from villages.

5. Voluntary canvassers and organizers are needed. **THIS IS WHERE WOMEN'S INSTITUTES CAN BE PARTICULARLY HELPFUL.**

6. A noticeable site for a dump should be selected on a road that can be used by heavy lorries.

7. Notices (which the Iron and Steel Control will supply) should be put near the dump and in all places commonly used for public notices. Householders and farmers in and around the village should be personally canvassed.

8. Obsolete iron and steel articles of all kinds are required—old stoves, flat irons, bedsteads, obsolete tools, farm and garden implements, and machinery, old railings : things that at present wastefully clutter up yards, corners of fields, attics, and outhouses can be turned into valuable munitions of war.

9. When the dump contains a worthwhile load—three or four tons—the local organizer should inform the Iron and Steel Control, **which will arrange for the dump to be cleared.**

10. Standard prices have been laid down by the Government, and profits made out of the Iron and Steel Control's village collection scheme will be handed to the Red Cross Agricultural Fund.

If a scrap iron and steel collection scheme has not yet been started in your village, write at once to the Iron and Steel Control at the address given above and get one going.

aged 28, son of Tom and Lydia Barlow and husband of Beryl Lilian Barlow of Castle Acre, Norfolk. He is commemorated on Portsmouth Naval Memorial, Hampshire.

Rev. Frank Burnett, Chaplain, HMS *Barham*, Royal Naval Volunteer Reserve was killed on 25 November 1941. His ship HMS *Barham* had an illustrious history in battle, having served in the First World War in the North Sea before being modernized and sent to the Atlantic and Mediterranean in the Second World War. She was torpedoed in December 1939, engaged the *Richelieu* in September 1940, took part in the Battle of Cape Matapan in March 1941 and was damaged by bombing in May. On 25 November 1941 the *U-331* hit her with three torpedoes, her magazines exploded and she sank in moments with the loss of more than two thirds of her crew.

David Burrows, Able Seaman, was on board the HMS *Juno* when she was attacked by a German Junkers Ju 88 bomber and died on 21 May 1941. He was aged 21 and the son of Claude and Elizabeth Burrows of Caister on Sea. He has no known grave and is commemorated on Chatham Naval Memorial.

A fine collection of metal pots and pans, St Giles Street, Norwich.

A B17C burnt out on take-off, 7 December 1941.

Peace *sheathing her sword: sculpture in Norwich to the men of the Norfolk Regiment who fought in the Boer War.*

Edward George Clarke, Able Seaman C/JX 155761 on HMS *Calcutta*, Royal Navy, died on Sunday, 1 June 1941, aged 18 years. He was the son of Cyril and Ethel May Clarke of Mundesley, Norfolk. He is commemorated on Chatham Naval Memorial, Kent.

Alfred Arthur Flint, Aircraftman 2nd Class 1251995, 901 Balloon Squadron, Royal Air Force Volunteer Reserve, died 12 January 1941, aged 33. He was the son of Arthur Clayton and Minnie Eliza Flint of Hunstanton. He is buried in New Hunstanton Cemetery.

Victor Robert Francis, Leading Stoker P/K 59651, HMS *Hood*, Royal Navy, died 24 May 1941, aged 38, when HMS *Hood* exploded and sunk while engaged with the *Bismarck* in the Denmark Strait. There were only 3 survivors and over 1,400 men were lost. Victor Francis was the son of Charles and Ellen Francis and husband of Lydia Francis of Burnham Norton, Norfolk. He is commemorated on Portsmouth Naval Memorial.

Joseph Walter Jackson, Telegraphist P/JX 215221, HMS *Dunedin*, Royal Navy, died 24 November 1941, aged 25. This 'D' Class Cruiser was north east of Recife, Brazil, when she was sunk by two torpedoes from submarine *U-124*. Joseph Jackson was the son of Percy and May Jackson of Downham Market, Norfolk. He is commemorated on Portsmouth Naval Memorial, Hampshire.

Francis Albert Lewis, Leading Seaman C/JX 142180 HMS *Exmoor*, Royal Navy, died on 25 February 1941, aged 22. He was the son of Francis and Elizabeth Lewis of Cley-next-the Sea, Norfolk and has no known grave. He is commemorated on Chatham Naval Memorial. Note: HMS *Exmoor* was sunk by a submarine off Lowestoft, Suffolk.

Jean Edie Pitchers, Civilian War Dead, aged 7, died 11 April 1941, in North Quay Shelter, Great Yarmouth. She was the daughter of Harold and Nora Edis Pitchers of 45 North Quay.

Margaret Eileen Pitchers, Civilian War Dead, aged 2 months, died 11 April 1941 in North Quay Shelter, Great Yarmouth. She was the daughter of Harold and Nora Edis Pitchers of 45 North Quay.

Nora Edis Pitchers, Civilian War Dead, aged 27, died 11 April 1941 in North Quay Shelter, Great Yarmouth. She was the wife of Harold Pitcher of 45 North Quay.

Patricia Ann Pitchers, Civilian War Dead, aged 2, died 11 April 1941 in North Quay Shelter, Great Yarmouth. She was the daughter of Harold and Nora Edis Picher of 45 North Quay.

Christopher Dermont Salmond Smith D.F.C., Squadron Leader, 79 Squadron, Royal Air Force, died 22 December 1941, aged 25. He was awarded the Distinguished Flying Cross. He was the son of Matthew and Mary Smith of Overy Staithe, Norfolk. He is commemorated on Runneymede Memorial.

James Clifford Tufts, Petty Officer D/J 107649 HMS *Galatea*, died 15 December 1941, aged 33, when his ship was sunk by a

LOSS OF H.M.S. HOOD.

SKETCHES BY CAPTAIN J.C. LEACH, M.V.O., ROYAL NAVY, SHOWING THE APPEARANCE AND POSITION OF THE EXPLOSION WHICH DESTROYED THE SHIP AS SEEN FROM H.M.S. PRINCE OF WALES AT A DISTANCE OF 4 CABLES.

Hand-drawn view of the loss of the Hood.

German submarine near Alexandria with the loss of 470 lives. He was the son of Sidney and Ellen Tufts of Southery, Norfolk. He has no known grave and is commemorated on Plymouth Naval Memorial.

HMS Barham *exploding.*

HMS Barham *refuelling.*

HMS Dunedin.

CHAPTER FOUR

1942

At A Glance: Local and World events

JANUARY

Local

Bitterly cold weather hampers farmers. Invasion committees are warned that heavy attacks continue to be possible on East Anglia. Great Yarmouth Council asks Whitehall for financial help and is refused.

World

In Washington a twenty-six nation pact is signed. Japanese forces invade Burma.

FEBRUARY

Local

Arctic weather and snow continues. A drive is started to persuade residents on Norfolk coast to voluntarily leave homes. East Anglian farmers in revolt at price proposals. Norfolk troops are reported as being in action in Malaya.

World

Nazi puppet government set up in Norway. *Scharnhorst* escapes from Brest. Battle of Java.

MARCH

Local

Attacks on East Coast. Huge construction of aerodromes in East Anglia.

World

Japanese take Rangoon. Allies surrender in Java.

APRIL

Local

Baedeker raids begin. 'Hot Pie' scheme introduced. Ban on public access to coast.

World

Japan bombs India. Japanese sink more UK shipping.

MAY

Local

Anglican cathedral damaged. Rumours take hold of invasion in Norfolk.

World

Anglo-Soviet Treaty signed. First 1,000 bomber raid by RAF.

JUNE

Local

Big battle exercises in East Anglia. King and Queen visit area.

World

US successes against Japan. Tobruk falls.

JULY

Local

Americans begin to arrive in Norfolk. Plea to farmers to use Land Girls.

World

US Air Force attacks European targets. British advance in Egypt.

AUGUST

Local

'Stay at Home' holiday scheme. All hands to harvest including Italians.

SEPTEMBER

Local

USAAF planes arrive in Norfolk. What to do with the Italian prisoners?

World

Heavy Russian and RAF bombing raids.

OCTOBER

Local

Large-scale evacuation exercises in East Anglia.

World

US launch biggest ever daylight raid of war on Lille. Japanese and British both go on offensive.

NOVEMBER

Local

Visit by Mrs Eleanor Roosevelt. First list of East Anglian prisoners in Far East received.

World

British breakthrough in Egypt. Axis armies enter Vichy France. Russian offensive begins in Caucasus.

DECEMBER

Local

Norfolk children's parties held at American bases. Farmers told to increase production again.

World

Axis armies retreat in Libya. British and Indian troops advance into Burma.

> *'It is always impolite to criticize your hosts. It is militarily stupid to criticize your Allies.'*
>
> From A Short Guide to Great Britain, issued to troops by the US War Department

Early disasters and life at home

Can You Take It?

> *It's easy to be nice, boys*
> *When everything's O.K.*
> *It's easy to be cheerful,*
> *When you're having things your way.*
> *But can you hold your head up*
> *And take it on the chin.*
> *When your heart is breaking*
> *And you feel like giving in?*

Anonymous

There is possibly no other time in history when Britain suffered such a series of serious defeats as at the beginning of 1942. Japan followed the bombing of the American Fleet with campaigns in Malaya, Hong Kong, the Philippines, Burma and Borneo. On 21 January Rommel began an advance in North

Africa towards the airfields that were vital to the defence of Malta. The German battleships *Scharnhorst* and *Gneisenau*, which had been blockaded in Brest, escaped and sailed through the Straits of Dover to safety. Singapore fell to the Japanese on 15 February: those captured included the 18th Division in which were men from battalions of the Royal Norfolks and the Suffolk, Cambridgeshire, and Beds and Herts regiments. The East Anglian families were told a series of half truths about what had happened to their menfolk. They had to glean what they could from inadequate news reports, mostly taken from enemy sources due to the restrictions imposed on home news. From 21 February the local press carried a regular feature 'Missing in Malaya'. Mutual support groups were established to give what comfort and support was possible to members. In February, recognizing the extreme practical needs of servicemen's families, the government increased the Servicemen's allowance to 3s 6d a week.

Morale could be low, although it was claimed by some that workers in the rural parts of Norfolk had never had it so good – their pay was fine, there was no shortage of food and, unless a bomb dropped or an aeroplane crashed, there was no need to think of the war at all. In towns, however, there was a shortage of many things, including clothes (there was for a time a person with the title of 'Director General of Civilian Clothing') and the buses were painted 'battleship grey' when necessary on account of the shortage of coloured paint. There were still jobs, though, especially for domestic workers and cars were easily available if you had the money.

Clothing rationing in 1942 was limited to forty-eight coupons a year. The President of the Board of Trade broadcast that while women could look smart, it was fine for men to look shabby – in fact it was a mark of honour. So what could be obtained with the coupons? Here are a few examples:

For men, raincoat 16 coupons, 11 for a child; overalls, 6, 4 for a child; pyjamas 8, 6 for a child; shirt, 4, 2 for a child; pants 4, 2 for a child; and shoes 7, 3 for a child.

For women, raincoat 14, 11 for a child; dress, 11, 8 for a child; dungarees 6, 4 for a child; pyjamas 8, 6 for a child; undergarments 3, 2 for a child; and slippers or shoes 5, 3 for a child.

This was also the time of the spiv, subsequently immortalized in films and popular TV programmes like *Dad's Army*. He is usually portrayed as a too well-dressed individual, able to get hold of anything for a price. They undoubtedly existed, especially in Norfolk after the Americans came with sweets, cigarettes, nylons and all manner of luxury goods and could often be seen making deals in the local pubs. The public had an ambivalent attitude to them.

Much was about to change in the airfields of East Anglia with the imminent arrival of the American servicemen and massive building of airfields. The new de Havilland Mosquito fighters came into action from January and were to have a decisive effect in protecting Norwich in the forthcoming blitz. The army, too, was at a new strength – 2,250,000 men plus 900,000 more from the Commonwealth while the Home Guard numbered 1,500,000.

Evacuation plans and invasion exercises

As Churchill faced a vote of confidence in the Commons, new plans were drawn up for compulsory evacuation in the event of an invasion. The latest thinking was that it would probably be the coasts of Suffolk and southward, not Norfolk, that would see most landings of enemy forces. Great Yarmouth was one Norfolk town where every person was to be evacuated, along with about a dozen in Suffolk. Meanwhile, efforts at encouraging voluntary evacuation were to be maintained, especially as some of the inhabitants of coastal settlements who had originally travelled inland had decided to move back to their homes. Plans were also drawn up to move patients from hospitals to free up 170,000 beds for invasion casualties. Captured enemy soldiers would be sent first to Newmarket and then to Wales where they would be kept in 'command cages'.

Alongside the issuing of such plans a series of full-scale 'invasion exercises' were undertaken involving every branch of Civil Defence and the police. Coastal communities had the additional exercises of repelling invasion from the sea. 'Results' varied in that sometimes the 'invaders' reached, perhaps the Town Hall (even in the case of King's Lynn, capturing the Mayor, Mr H.W. Watling, who pronounced the whole exercise the greatest success) or took over the hospitals and sometimes they were beaten back by the 'defenders'; always realistic scenarios were created with people wounded under branches, confused members of the public wandering all over and gas and water mains ruptured. Tear Gas was released in the narrow Rows (Alleyways) of Great Yarmouth and several elderly people had to rush into nearby shops to breathe.

Inspection by the Prime Minister.

Norfolk Coast takes a battering;
Bombings of Great Yarmouth, King's Lynn and Sheringham

Visitors were not allowed on the coastal belt – just officially maybe, as a good few took the chance to get to the seashore and faced a fine if caught – and a large proportion of the population had left anyway, at least temporarily. This led to an impossible financial situation for many councils as they could hardly raise rates on empty businesses. Great Yarmouth sent a delegation to London in 1942 only to be told that they had to do the best they could and that no money was available to help them.

There was money, at least, to be derived from the fact that virtually all East Coast ports were busy naval bases and many had their own shops, canteens, clubs and even theatres, but the money circulating by these means rarely reached the outside communities.

The Germans made renewed efforts to lay mines along the East Coast utilizing the new, fast motor- torpedo boat named the *Schnellboot*. The British retaliated with improved minesweeping vessels, some coming from America. The East Coast was protected in early 1942 by six flotillas of motor gunboats, two motor-torpedo boats and eight motor launches. These ships would stay about 8 miles out from the shipping lanes on permanent standby. The RAF was there, too, but the first two months of 1942 nevertheless saw the sinking of thirteen ships and two destroyers.

A battle took place on the third weekend of March when a force of the *Schnellboot* – or E-boats as they were called for short – attacked an Allied convoy, the location of the fighting all the while moving from the Channel to the Norfolk coast. Spitfires joined in on the Sunday morning and several of the fast E-boats were sunk. HMS *Vortigern* was also fatally holed leading to the immediate launch of both the Sheringham and Cromer No 1 lifeboats even as the battle raged: only twelve men, all of them dead, were picked up.

The coast off Yarmouth was christened 'E-boat alley' over the summer and autumn and in December the Germans

Training exercise on the Norfolk Broads.

managed to sink five ships in one convoy. Many of the ships sailing this coast were laden with coal as it was intended to stockpile huge reserves in southern England.

The Sheringham lifeboat was once again in action in October when it picked up six Polish airmen who were seen precariously

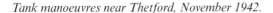

Tank manoeuvres near Thetford, November 1942.

Exercises on Norfolk canals.

floating on the wreckage of their aircraft. This is now the stuff of legend in the area as the RNLI secretary apparently conducted rescue operations by telephone from his bed onshore, not having time to get dressed. He made or received twenty-one telephone messages in twenty-six minutes, even arranging for hot baths to be ready for the crew in private Sheringham homes.

The Germans were unrelenting in attacking the East Coast. Often it was opportunistic and with just one plane. On 18 February seven people were killed as two houses were destroyed and then, just after midday, a lone bomber dropped four bombs: as often happened, people rushed out to see what was happening and many were killed and buried in the debris. Great Yarmouth almost never escaped and early on the morning of 30 May three people were killed in a bombing raid; on 10 June it was attacked with incendiaries and on 25 June huge damage was done to the Church of St Nicholas, the Spire collapsing, the

British Motor Gun Boat 314.

Spire was never rebuilt, although the clock to celebrate victory which was added to the tower in 1919 was unscathed, and so it can be seen today. It is a magnificent rebuilt church and claims, although one or two others in the UK also claim the same distinction, to be the largest parish church in the land.

'The bombing itself grows vague and dreamlike. The little pictures remain as sharp as they were when they were new.'

John Steinbeck

HMS Vortigern *during the Great War.*

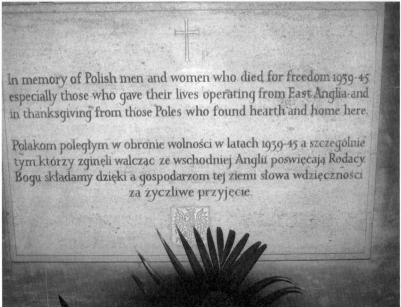

In memory of Polish men and women who died for freedom 1939-45 especially those who gave their lives operating from East Anglia and in thanksgiving from those Poles who found hearth and home here.

Polakom poległym w obronie wolności w latach 1939-45 a szczególnie tym którzy zginęli walcząc ze wschodniej Anglii poświęcają Rodacy. Bogu składamy dzięki a gospodarzom tej ziemi słowa wdzięczności za życzliwe przyjęcie.

Shrine in the Cathedral of St John the Baptist to the Polish men and women who came to Norwich during the war.

The Roman Catholic Cathedral, Norwich.

King's Lynn was attacked twice in June. In the early light of the 12th a lone Dornier was responsible for the deaths of seventeen civilians and a number of service personnel. The Eagle hotel and nearby premises were destroyed. On 30 June five bombs lodged in the roof of King Edward VII Grammar School, masters and boarders – who had gone to bed – rushing out onto the roof to douse the flames. The dormitories where dozens of boys had been sleeping were burnt out.*

*The author was a boarder at King Edward VII Grammar School many years later, and slept in the rebuilt dormitories for the six years of his secondary education. We boys knew of this tale, of course, and many times tried to work out how it was possible to get onto the roof from our dormitories. It was not: the only way would have been if the walls of the dormitories and adjacent washrooms had been blasted out, which was quite possible. The only other way was through the circular stairs off the main hall of the school, via the Geography room – this was proved when several boarders were caught on the school roof in their pyjamas at 3 in the morning.

St Nicholas Church in Great Yarmouth, without the spire which was felled by a bomb in 1942 and never replaced. The clock survives and was put there in 1919 to celebrate victory in the Great War.

The following day there was an attack on a hospital and on the docks. There were fourteen air raid alerts on the August Bank Holiday. One of the wardens records seeing a bomber flying low and slow over defenceless crowds of men, women and children. It declined to fire – had it done so, scores would have been killed.

Sheringham was dive-bombed on 27 July and nine killed while a raid on Great Yarmouth on 29 killed two. Great Yarmouth and Cromer were attacked again in October. The last raid on Norfolk in 1942 was on 22 December when a single hit-and-run raider flew over several areas, Great Yarmouth bearing the brunt of the loss of life – six – and damage. The plane was shot down.

By the year's end Great Yarmouth had been bombed twenty-six times, with twenty-seven killed and ninety-five injured. Sirens and 'crash warnings' totalled 615.

Following bombing in 1942 (above), the Church of St Nicholas was magnificently restored (top).

Revolving library and pulpit destroyed by bombs in St Nicholas Church, Great Yarmouth, 1942.

Baedeker Blitz. Three raids in a week; more raids

The Baedeker Guides began in 1827, and quickly became indispensable to many world travellers. The first was of the Rhine and was apparently produced to save tourists having to pay a personal guide. They gained a reputation for thoroughness – Karl Baedeker was once seen climbing the steps of Milan Cathedral, placing a coin on every twentieth step so that his count would be accurate. In 1942 Exeter, Bath, York, Canterbury and Norwich were all selected for maximum damage because, in the words of Baron Gustav Von Sturm, 'We shall go out and bomb every building in Britain marked with three stars in the Baedeker guide.' Allied bombers were to destroy the company's HQ in Leipzig the following year.*

There were three raids in one week. The first was on the clear moonlit night of Monday, 27/28 April. At 11.40 two pathfinder planes dropped parachute flares and then incendiary bombs on the city centre, starting an uncontrollable fire over 120 acres – the epicentre was the Midland and Great Northern Joint Railway's City Station. Twenty-six more aircraft arrived dropping high explosives – estimated later at 185 bombs – and incendiaries in an attack that lasted sixty-five minutes. Norwich Social Welfare Institution in Bowthorpe Road was hit. Nine of the hundreds of elderly patients were killed, the rest being moved in time to the shelters. The Norwich Institute for the Blind was also hit but with no casualties. Other buildings damaged included the Regal Cinema – roof blown off; the Hippodrome Theatre; some of the city's leading stores – Curl's (later Debenhams), Woolworths, Boots, Buntings; the shoe factories of Bowhill and Hubbard and Edwards and Holme's; Coleman's Wincarnis factory; and the Norwich Union offices. Lord Haw Haw, the infamous pro-German broadcaster, predicted the destruction of the new City Hall but this did not happen. The anti-aircraft guns stopped firing as RAF fighters arrived.

*The guides have been revised and reissued in the past decade. By 1942 Norwich had already been bombed twenty-seven times with eighty-one killed and many more injured. The Baedeker raids, however, were on a different scale.

The corner of Surrey Street in peacetime.

The corner of Surrey Street, Norwich after a bomb attack. Row & Taylor later became the site of Marks & Spencer.

A shot of the same spot today.

Norwich City Station after direct hits.

The greatest destruction was to private dwellings. Civil Defence mobilized immediately and a special mention was, in the aftermath, made of the messenger service, boys of sixteen to eighteen, who rode through the bombs to deliver vital messages, some of them being blown from their machines only to get up

'Lord Hee-Haw, Chief Wind-Bag' from a 1943 animated film.

Curl Brothers, Norwich, about 1939 looking up to St Peter Mancroft (centre).

Looking up to St Peter Mancroft today.

and carry on. One, made a hero at the time, was John David Grix who was only fifteen but had lied about his age in order to volunteer. The Church Army, Women's Voluntary Service and YMCA all worked through the night moving the injured, rescuing what could be saved, providing clothing and making meals and, of course, tea – some diaries of the time remark humorously on how good were the spirits of the survivors given a cup of tea. As dawn broke, postmen, papermen and milkmen went to work as usual only to sometimes find row-upon-row of working people's houses no longer there. Queues formed around City Hall to find out if there was any news regarding missing loved ones.

Some 162 people died and over 600 were injured in this first Baedeker raid. Many decided to sleep in the countryside for the immediate future, the sight of the scared and destitute subsequently hobbling out of the city in the evening and then back again in the morning making a pitiful sight, according to the *Eastern Daily Press*. The city had a pungent aroma caused by pouring tons of water onto burning wood and clouds of dust drifted slowly above the wreckage.

On Wednesday, 29/30, the same pattern of raid was repeated as the bombers flew under the anti-aircraft guns and dropped flares, bombs and incendiaries at low altitude followed by machine-gunning of streets as they came out of their dives. This was a seventy-five minute raid and the new Mosquitos from RAF Castle Camps took to battle for the first time.

Some 112 high explosive bombs were dropped and damage was severe. A.J. Caley's factory, where Chapelfield Shopping Centre was later built, was gutted by flames releasing liquid chocolate onto the streets. Other buildings destroyed or badly hit included Norwich Diocesan Training College, Clarke's shoe factory, St Mary's Silk Mills, the Barker Engineering Company works and the Hippodrome Theatre. A locally well-known story about the theatre tells of a seal called 'Buddy', part of one of the variety acts, who was apparently in the devastated building but members of his touring company found him hale and hearty the next morning, none the worse for his experiences. Some pubs and churches also suffered damage.

The Fire Service – the site subsequently became a school.

The Fire Station today.

City Hall and Breath by Paul de Monchaux, commissioned by Norwich City Council in 2010; 'The Living Honour the Dead. Only a Breath Divides Them'.

A Norwich home following an attack – note the bedstead is still there in the upstairs room.

Fighting the fires.

The centre of Norwich showing Caley's factory just prior to bombing. The site later became the Chapelfield Shopping Centre.

Site being attacked.

Above and following pages: scenes of destruction in Norwich.

The third attack of the week's raids began at 1.35 am on Friday, 1 May. This time only one plane got through but dropped a container which scattered 700 explosive incendiaries over the city causing multiple fires. Fireguards quickly brought the fires under control, however.

Reports of the time mention a few things repeatedly – the ear-splitting noise of the bombings; the smell of smoke, dust and charred wood and stone; the lack of washing facilities and water which resulted in a dirty, dishevelled populace; the cheerfulness and tea drinking; and the determination from everyone – milkmen, office workers, women with tots-in-arms and others – just to carry on as normally as possible. Some of this was, of course, propaganda, as the local press was not able initially to release the true extent of the damage. Unfortunately, nothing could be done to stop people gossiping: morale was harmed by rumours of destruction in places that had, in fact, escaped the raids and all sorts of other horrors that had not occurred.

The dead were buried on 4, 5 and 6 May in a mass grave with full civic and religious honours.

The local stores opened wherever they could – Bonds, for example, utilized fourteen different locations around the city as well as selling from buses; Jarrold and Garlands offered their floor space to Curl's and others.

Men on top of bombed building, Orford Place, Norwich.

The Cathedral Church of Holy and Undivided Trinity in the Close, the jewel in the crown of Norwich, so to speak, suffered only relatively minor damage to some windows. St Peter Mancroft's damage was similar. St Benedict's, St Bartholomew at Heigham and St Anne's on the Earlham Estate were destroyed.

Several pubs were destroyed, including the fifteenth-century Boar's Head in St Stephen's Street.

Names are today still being added to memorials and lists of those who died. In March 2017 four former policemen were

Bells fallen to the floor in St Bartholomew's Church, Norwich April 1942.

Riverside destruction, Norwich 1942.

The YMCA provides tea after the blitz.

remembered and their names added to the roll at Bethel Street Police Station. They are Arthur Pennymore, 55, of Bracondale who died on 2 December 1940; Arthur Wilby, 35, who was killed on 27 June 1942 – his wife, Kate, was also injured; George Smith, 43, of Patteson Road who died of shrapnel on 5 September 1942 in Magdalen Street; and Sam Bussey, 33, who was killed fighting fires in Oak Street on 28 April 1942. Ronald and Ken, sons of George Smith, were able to attend the ceremony.

More raids followed, the first being just after midnight on 9 May. However, defences were

A tearful moment for a mother and her children.

Two famous Americans who came to Norfolk. Jimmy Stewart (l) served
at Tibenham, where, in 2012, Stewart Close was named after him, and Old
Buckenham. Local folklore has it that Glenn Miller (r) dropped unannounced
into the King George V pub, south of Norwich, and played the piano in 1944.

greatly improved. Thirty-five barrage balloons were quickly
raised while the newly installed heavy anti-aircraft guns and
thirty-seven sorties by the RAF rendered precision bombing
of the city impossible. Most of the bombs fell outside the city
causing little damage.

A raid on the night of 26/27 June caused sixteen deaths
and many injuries. The operation was similar to all the others
– flares, incendiaries and bombs – and the roof and one wing
of the Norfolk and Norwich Hospital were burnt out. Patients
were evacuated to the lawns from where they watched the attack.

The Anglican Cathedral roof was hit again with incendiaries
during this attack and timbers set ablaze. The Cathedral was
probably saved by the bravery of two fireguards who clambered

After the bombing of Bonds department store, the management took to selling goods to the public from buses.

up to the roof and dealt with the fire. Bonds the drapers was burnt out, too.

Another raid that did little damage occurred during the early morning of 28 July; then others on 2 August, 13 August, 5 September, 19 October, 3 November and 5 December. The raid on 5 September was on a busy Saturday morning with people shopping and six were killed.

All Saints Green, Norwich, site of Bonds Department Store, now John Lewis.

By the end of 1942, Norwich had had 106 alerts, 2,082 dwellings had been demolished and 30,000 badly damaged. Repair work was co-ordinated using a plan drawn up by Norwich City Engineer, Mr H. C. Rowley, who had seen for himself the results of the blitz on Coventry. Each part of the city was 'allocated' a

All Saints Green, Norwich, today.

master builder who set repairs in motion immediately. Compulsory powers were applied to draft in workers, many of whom came from London – they were christened 'Cockney Sparrows'. MAGNA – the Mutual Aid Good Neighbours' Association – was set up to offer help, food, warmth, clothing and organize accommodation to those who were temporarily bombed out: they were very effective indeed, 30,000 Norwich women signing up as 'a good neighbour', putting a small yellow sticker in their front windows.

The Deputy Chief Constable received an MBE and four British Empire Medals were given to those who helped with the damage. The cyclist-messenger already mentioned, 15-year-old John David Grix, was one so honoured and he took a trip with his parents to Buckingham Palace. As he was mobbed, he is reported as saying: 'Look here, this is a jolly sight worse than any blitz.'

David Grix meets the King, 13 October 1942.

Retaliation

'They sowed the wind, and now they are going to reap the whirlwind.'

Air Chief Marshal Sir Arthur Harris

The RAF Bomber Command carried out a steady programme of raids on Germany during 1942. The most memorable, as far as the population of Norfolk was concerned was the force of a thousand aircraft sent to Cologne on 30 May under the orders of Air Chief Marshal Sir Arthur Harris. On their way, this massive fleet passed over Norfolk, and in particular Cromer and Great Yarmouth, two of the coastal towns that had suffered some of the worst German attacks of the war. Witnesses came out of their homes to see the sky almost black with Wellingtons and Stirlings from East Anglian and other bases. The raid lasted 90 minutes and 3,000 tons of bombs were dropped. It was the biggest attack of the war so far.

At Home in Norfolk: need for workers, shopping, duty, women, conscientious objectors, child labour and the Italians

Workers of every kind were becoming scarce now. Despite appeals, seven men between the ages of twenty-one and thirty-three who manned the two Cromer lifeboats were called up: this despite the fact that the two boats had been launched 116 times since the start of the war and that most of the men remaining were approaching seventy. Henry Blogg, recent recipient of his Third RNLI Gold Medal and a national hero following his exploits in both world wars, declared his unhappiness but, perhaps typically, added '….we shall have to do the best we can'.

Shoppers were told to take their own goods home with them and not rely on delivery and this meant paying on the spot, not relying on credit. Clothes became more utilitarian and it

Cromer Lifeboat H.F. Bailey, *now restored in museum.*

Saxone shoe shop in Norwich.

Prince of Wales Road, 1930s.

A shot of the above scene today.

Women's Land Army girls at Norwich Cathedral.

actually became illegal to decorate underwear with lace or other frills. 'Utility' everything started to appear for sale – furniture, cutlery, clocks, watches, pencils, cigarette lighters, can openers, vases, corsets, trousers, shoes, hats and wedding rings.

In Norfolk and other areas considered vulnerable, enrolment in the Home Guard became compulsory from March 1942. All men between the ages of eighteen and sixty were registered for duty in some form or another.

Women were increasingly vital, especially to farming and the still thriving Norwich shoe industry. They were also bus drivers and conductors, mail delivery staff and telephone engineers (who were paid the good sum of 41s to 59 6d). Women were also increasingly entering the armed forces but this caused some resentment against undergraduates and other young men seen living a comfortable life in the region's towns.

Conscientious objectors regularly came before Norwich courts and their reception was far from hostile. The cause of those who could not find it in their conscience to harm another or fight had gained wider acceptance during the Great War and now it was no different. Providing a person was prepared to do some non-combatant service, they could be excused: refusal almost certainly meant prison.

From January 1942 boys aged seventeen were also required to register so that they could be called up quickly if needed, and then, next month, boys of sixteen. At the beginning of the year, the age of actual call up was averaging eighteen and a half and, by the end, eighteen. The Army Cadet Force was set up to train those even younger. An Air Training Corps and a Sea Cadet Corps were also formed. Girls had a Girls' Training Corps for those aged between fourteen and eighteen.

Children were also required for the harvest: those aged twelve or over were allowed to work not more than twenty school sessions in one year and never more than seven hours in a day. This was hugely controversial, the Norfolk man heading the National Union of Agricultural Workers, Mr Edward

Norfolk pie scheme in operation.

Gooch, declaring it 'a crime against children'.

More men and women were expected to attend fire-fighting groups – anyone under forty-five of either sex who failed to volunteer or turn up when needed was liable to prosecution.

There was one new source of labour – Italian prisoners of war. They were already known in Norfolk but, from May 1942, they arrived in batches of 5,000, two thirds of whom were directed to agriculture. The rest were given work as tradesmen or labourers. Initially they were put into camps but increasingly those deemed of 'good conduct' were allowed to live on the farms. By the end of the year there were 8,000 working in the Eastern Command. They were often disliked at first as their English was not good but needs must and they became much more highly valued as the conflict went on.

Food, dried egg, and rationing; some war recipes for the home front; The Haybox

British Restaurants, already mentioned, were having a noticeable effect in the towns by producing nutritious and good-value meals. In the countryside, of which Norfolk had a great deal, a 'Pies Scheme' was introduced. Rural councils were asked to produce and deliver pies to workers at lunchtime. Thousands were delivered every day, using ex-War department vehicles, and were priced at four pence each.

Simultaneously, school meals were increased in number.

LORD WOOLTON PIE

THE OFFICIAL RECIPE

In hotels and restaurants, no less than in communal canteens, many people have tasted Lord Woolton pie and pronounced it good. Like many another economical dish, it can be described as wholesome fare. It also meets the dietician's requirements in certain vitamins. The ingredients can be varied according to the vegetables in season. Here is the official recipe: —

Take 1lb. each diced of potatoes, cauliflower, swedes, and carrots, three or four spring onions—if possible, one teaspoonful of vegetable extract, and one tablespoonful of oatmeal. Cook all together for 10 minutes with just enough water to cover. Stir occasionally to prevent the mixture from sticking. Allow to cool; put into a piedish, sprinkle with chopped parsley, and cover with a crust of potato or wheatmeal pastry. Bake in a moderate oven until the pastry is nicely browned and serve hot with a brown gravy.

The Ministry of Food had much to say to the general population. 'Food Facts' and recipes were produced in all Norfolk newspapers. Norfolk had particular blessings in food production, including potatoes, turnips, apples and vegetables and, unsurprisingly, the *East Anglian Daily Times* carried recipes for Potato and Watercress Soup and Turnip Top Salad. In June an additional pound of sugar per person was allowed for jam making as the fruit crop was very good. On 24 June a new substance came from America, Canada and Argentina – dried egg. Every two months each person could have one tin – about the equivalent of twelve eggs. Lord Woolton said it was simply 'egg minus water and shell'. Many disagreed, not taking to it at all, but not enough to turn it down.

At the end of the year, the government was able to offer free cod liver oil and vitamin orange juice to young children and mothers-to-be. In Norwich, hundreds regularly queued in front of City Hall for their supplies.

War recipes for the home front

Lord Woolton Pie

This is probably the most famous Second World War recipe. It was reputedly created at the Savoy Hotel, London by Francis Latry. It was named after Lord Woolton who became Minister of Food in 1940. It contains no meat.

Ingredients

1lb each of potato, spring onion, cauliflower or cabbage, carrot, swede, 1 teaspoon Marmite or similar, tablespoon oatmeal. Other vegetables can be substituted which, in Norfolk, would probably include peas as crops reached record levels, especially in 1944 and 1945.

For the pastry: 6oz flour, 1½oz butter, 1½oz lard, 2oz raw potatoes.

Method

Wash, peel and chop all vegetables. Add Marmite and oatmeal. Put in pan and cover with water. Simmer until soft – about 15 minutes.

Separately put flour, butter and lard in bowl. Mix until it resembles breadcrumbs. Grate and add the raw potato. Add small quantity of water and make into pastry.

Grease a pie dish and put vegetables into it. Put pastry over the top. Pierce pastry in several places to allow steam to escape. Brush pastry with milk or beaten egg if available.

Put into moderate oven for about half an hour.

Serve with gravy.

Almost Fishless Cakes

Ingredients

5oz boiled potatoes or rice, lemon juice, 2 teaspoons of fish stock or any left-over pieces of fish, pepper, 2oz flour. Many people on the Norfolk coast would be able to buy some mackerel or kippers and this recipe would help the food go much further than just cooking the fish.

Method

Mix all together and form into cakes. Fry and serve with vegetables or salad.

Rabbit stew

Ingredients

1 rabbit, cut into joints, 1oz flour, seasoning, 1-2oz fat, 2 chopped bacon rashers if available, 2 onions and 3 carrots chopped, 1 pint water, 1 grated apple.

Method

Soak rabbit in cold water for 30 minutes. Dry. Mix flour and seasoning and coat rabbit joints. Fry the rabbit joints and bacon in the fat until golden. Put all ingredients in pan and simmer gently until rabbit cooked and tender, about 45 minutes.

Serve with Norfolk peas and carrots.

Eggless Cake

Ingredients

1lb self-raising flour, a quarter teaspoon of salt, 4oz margarine or butter, 4oz sugar, 14oz of fruit – currants, sultanas, orange or lemon peel, half a pint of milk, one quarter pint of water.

Method

Sieve flour into basin and rub in margarine. Add other ingredients and beat thoroughly. Put mixture into 8 inch greased tin and bake in medium oven for one and a half hours.

Dried egg on toast

Ingredients

Reconstituted egg, water, bread and margarine.

Method

Mix egg with a little water, according to instructions on tin, put into pan and fry for a few minutes until golden brown on both sides. Make toast and spread with margarine. Add egg to toast and eat immediately.

Oatmeal Cheese and Tomato Rarebit

Ingredients

1oz grated cheese, half an ounce of oatmeal, one chopped tomato, salt and pepper, chopped parsley or coriander, 1oz flour, quarter pint of water, toast and margarine.

Method

Make a sauce with the flour, oatmeal and water, add the cheese and tomato, salt and pepper and stir. Put onto toast and grill. Garnish with parsley or coriander.

This recipe is just for one person. Other things can be added to the cheese, for example, diced onion, peas or cooked chopped potatoes.

Potato Jane

Ingredients

1½lbs of potatoes, 3oz grated cheese, 2oz breadcrumbs, half a chopped small onion or leek, one sliced carrot, half a pint water, salt and pepper.

Method

Layer the ingredients in a greased oven dish, finishing with the cheese and breadcrumbs. Pour over the milk and bake in a medium oven for 45 minutes.

Potato Milk Pudding

Ingredients

1lb of shredded or finely chopped potato, 1oz flour, 1 pint of milk and water mix, 2 tablespoons jam, nutmeg.

Method

Heat the milk/water mix and flour to simmering point and mix with potato. Put everything into greased pie dish and cook in a low oven for one and a half hours.

Potato sandwich spreads

Ingredients

Cooked and mashed potato plus:

For sweet spreads, sugar and cocoa powder or fruit such as mashed apple. Use instead of jam.

For savoury spreads, salt and pepper and chopped vegetables or left-over meat. Put in sandwiches or on toast and grill.

Carrot biscuits

Ingredients

1 tablespoon of margarine/butter, 1 tablespoon sugar, vanilla essence, four tablespoons grated carrots, six tablespoons flour – self-raising or add half teaspoon baking powder.

Method

Cream the margarine/butter and sugar, beat in vanilla essence and carrot, fold in flour and make into biscuits. Cook in medium oven for about fifteen to twenty minutes.

Orange Golden Slices

Ingredients

Any stale bread cut into pieces, equivalent of two reconstituted eggs (see instructions on tin or just mix with a little water until 'eggy') grated orange or lemon peel, tablespoon orange or other fruit juice, fat for frying.

Method

Put bread in bowl and leave to soak up the ingredients, apart from the fat. Fry until golden and eat immediately.

Just as in the Great War, it was recommended that everyone construct or buy a haybox. This was a box filled with straw into which partially cooked food could be put in order to continue cooking. There could be several layers and then everything was packed inside a sealed container such as a tin. Huge amounts of fuel could be saved in this way if attention was paid to planning. Porridge, for example, could be heated for a few minutes before going to bed and then put in the haybox overnight.

German Haybox, late nineteenth century.

Make do and Mend, salvage drives and War Weeks

In Mid-March the existing clothing rationing system was reduced by a quarter, letters to the local press suggesting that in some cases underwear was so worn and threadbare as to be practically non-existent; 'Make do and Mend' was all very well, it was pointed out, provided you had something to work on!

On 30 June the basic petrol ration was withdrawn and bus services curtailed, especially on long routes.

A salvage campaign was undertaken – metal, bones, rags, rubber and, controversially, books which were divided up into reading matter for the Forces, valuable books and those for pulping. A Ministry of Information film doing the rounds to an enthusiastic public – hundreds turned up carrying waste paper in Norwich for the first viewing – was called 'Salvage with a Smile'.

The government sought also to encourage patriotism and, importantly, take money out of circulation (so there was less spending) by encouraging schemes for war savings. 'Warship Weeks' throughout the country combined a good day out with the opportunity to save for something tangible. Norwich

Bomb damage on corner of Guildhall Hill and Upper Goat Lane, Norwich 1942. This had been The Clover Leaf Milk Bar.

The rebuilt scene today.

NORWICH WARSHIP WEEK

JANUARY 31ˢᵗ TO FEBRUARY 7ᵗʰ 1942

OUR TARGET £1,000,000

NORWICH SAVINGS COMMITTEE,
SUCKLING HOUSE,
ST. ANDREW'S HILL,
NORWICH.
19th January, 1942

Dear Sir or Madam,

You will probably be aware that it has been decided to hold a Warship Week in Norwich from 31st January to 7th February.

The aim is to raise £1,000,000 through the various investments mentioned overleaf and the total will be devoted by His Majesty's Government towards the cost of a Warship.

A successful outcome to our efforts is only possible with your whole-hearted and enthusiastic support, and you are very strongly urged to invest to your utmost during the period and to persuade your friends and employees to render similar service.

Providing the financial target is reached the Admiralty will permit the "adoption" of H.M.S. "Norfolk" by the community and we feel that this will afford an additional incentive to enable our ambitious aim to be accomplished, whilst should you require any advice or assistance it will be readily forthcoming at the Selling Centres, included amongst which are the Branches of:

Barclays Bank, Ltd.	National Provincial Bank, Ltd.
Lloyds Bank, Ltd.	Westminster Bank, Ltd.
Midland Bank, Ltd.	Post Office Savings Bank.

East Anglian Trustee Savings Bank.

On behalf of the Committee, who appeal to you with every confidence for your maximum contribution to this portion of the National Effort,

Yours faithfully,

J. H. Barnes
Lord Mayor of Norwich.

Herbert W. Power
Chairman of Norwich Savings Committee.

GIVE THE NELSON TOUCH TO NORWICH WARSHIP WEEK

aimed to raise £1,000,000 to build a cruiser (the final figure was £1,392,649 which represented £11 for each person in the city); Ipswich asked the citizens for the same amount for a destroyer to be called HMS *Orwell*, in the end falling just short at £846,000; Great Yarmouth went for a lesser figure – £250,000 (it actually raised £300,000); King's Lynn for £120,000 'to pay for a corvette'; Thetford did not name a figure but managed to raise £50,000.

There were many other schemes which were less publicized such as 'Aid to Russia' and 'Prisoner of War Week'. Additionally, National Savings continued to be collected street by street. The money was sorely needed as Sir Kingsley Wood, the Chancellor of the Exchequer, announced that the cost of the war was £12,000,000 a day and Parliament had voted for only just over £10,000,000 in total since it began.

Clark Gable on duty in Norfolk.

Some news from Singapore

Families of men sent to face the Japanese had had a terrible time of it as news of their loved ones filtered through at best sporadically and briefly. At the end of November, the first official lists prepared by the Japanese of men taken prisoner at Singapore reached Britain. Around 1,900 smuggled-out postcards also reached home. Unfortunately, no Norfolk regiment was mentioned in the lists and the agonizing wait for families went on.

On 15 January 2015 the *Eastern Daily Press* reported that Beeston Regis centenarian, Len Fiske, one of the last surviving Second World War Royal Norfolk Regiment Far East Prisoners

American personnel off-duty.

of War, was celebrating his 100th birthday, seventy years after being liberated from the brutal Omi Japanese camp after being held for three years.

Yanks; a Christmas party in Lexham

The first Americans reached East Anglia in June – as they had not been announced people saw American airmen walking about in very fine uniforms before the local press utilized the Ministry of Information handouts welcoming them in August. There were problems – the US private received five times the two shillings a day that his British counterpart was paid; the men looked mighty finely dressed to people who were having to 'make do and mend' even their underwear; they often spoke first when that was not the expected custom, saying things like

GIs in Castle Meadow, Norwich.

'Howdy' in a cheerful voice; and some of them were black, the first non-Caucasians that a great many Norfolk people had seen. No wonder many local reports spoke of seeing American soldiers on their own, looking sad, especially in Norwich.

A law was passed whereby all criminal offences committed by the Americans were to be dealt with by the American court-martial procedure.

The US War Department handed each GI – the term 'GI' dates back to the Great War and actually originally meant 'Government Issue': In the Second World War it was the term used for an American soldier – a book of good advice containing both light-hearted and serious notes:

> The British don't know how to make a good cup of coffee. You don't know how to make a good cup of tea. It's an even swap. The British welcome you as friends and allies, but remember that crossing the ocean doesn't automatically make you a hero. There are housewives in aprons, and youngsters in knee-pants in Britain who have lived through more high explosives in air-raids than many soldiers saw in first-class barrages in the last war.....

Gradually things changed for the better as the Americans began fitting in: they organized a baseball game at Carrow Road, tried English (warm) beer and explained what hamburgers and 'pumpkin cream' were. Both the United States Ambassador, Mr John G. Winant and Mrs Eleanor Roosevelt, wife of the American President, visited Cambridge in October and November respectively.

GIs came laden with gifts for the girls – nylon stockings, chocolates and flowers. They held parties and laid on buses for the local ladies. To the resentment of some uniformed British lads, they seemed to sprinkle a little Hollywood stardust wherever they went. Nobody actually knew how many there were as the figures were top-secret. There certainly seemed to be a lot of them – over a thousand people, many of them from American bases, would crowd into the locally famous ballroom,

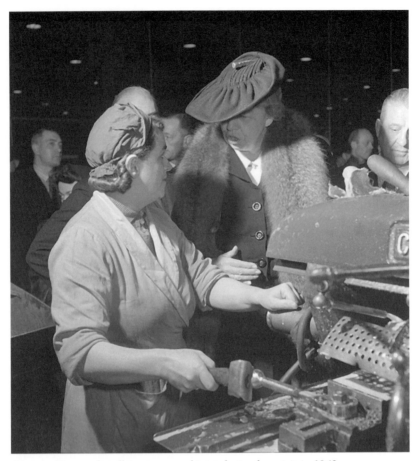

Eleanor Roosevelt talking to a machinist during her visit in 1942.

the Samson and Hercules, in Tombland (still there but later converted partly into flats). Norwich was not used to such glamour and excitement.

At Christmas over 400 Norwich homes offered hospitality to the new arrivals and, in return, the GIs put on parties for the youngsters with ice cream, jelly, gifts and a chance to sit in a Jeep or even a plane. Some GIs, missing home, wrote that this was the happiest time yet for them, even if they could barely hold their emotions in check as children clambered onto their laps. Toys, games, pens, pencils and much else arrived in their thousands from the United States and were distributed to schools and children's homes.

We have a contemporary and moving record of one Christmas party put on by the Americans for orphan boys and girls in Lexham. One of the airmen, Birdie Schmidt, tells the tale:

'We woke up to a white Christmas Day and a heavy hoar-frost covered the ground. The fog that went with it caused the (heavy bombing) mission to be cancelled. A party had been planned for 130 orphans and refugees from Dr Barnardo's Home for boys in Lexham and the Home Hale Village School children as well as those of our staff. The men on the base acted as hosts.

'The children were taken to the Perimeter where they had the opportunity to see inside a Liberator. This was quite a thrill for most of them as it was their first close-up view of an airplane. The GIs had their hands full in keeping order among the kids. The children were piled back into the trucks and brought to the theatre, which is next to the Aeroclub. They were greeted by the base orchestra which rendered several numbers. The children put on a programme of their own consisting of country dances, songs and recitations, and this really brought the house down. They did an excellent job and to see some of the smaller children breaking forth in song and dance was a sight to behold. The children were shown several movie cartoons, which they just loved.

'Throughout all this the children were climbing all over the laps of the GIs, and it tugged at my heart to see the expressions on the faces of the GIs. Perhaps it being my first Christmas with the GIs I didn't know what to expect, but it certainly did move me greatly to see their reactions to these underprivileged children

'After the movies, the children were brought to the Aeroclub and seated at long tables in the snack bar, which was decorated with packages of candy wrapped in red paper and holly and Christmas greens placed along the tables. We served tea, cakes and fruit jelly. We had planned to have ice cream but at the last moment the freezing unit broke down. It was late afternoon so we drew the blackout curtains and lit the candles, and Santa Claus came bursting into the room, much to the glee and shouts of the youngsters. One of the GIs acted as Father Christmas and did an excellent job. He went up onto the stage where the Christmas tree stood with piles of presents stacked around it. These presents were bought with money donated by the GIs. There were 130 presents – one for each child. When we counted noses, however, we had 160 children, so we scurried around and made 30 extra presents. Santa Claus read out each name and the GIs distributed the presents. With full stomachs and full of Christmas spirit the children got back into the trucks and were taken home.

'On Christmas night we played the recording of Dickens' 'A Christmas Carol' by Ronald Colman. There was free food in the snack bar: plum pudding with sauce, fudge, nuts and apples. Lots of GIs told me it was the best Christmas they had ever spent away from home.'

USAAF bases and planes

Alongside the change in society that came from the arrival of the GIs, Norfolk dramatically became a hive of construction activity. The older RAF bases in East Anglia were being given new concrete runways and in June the government approved construction of some new ones, including at Old Buckenham and Little Snoring in Norfolk. In July approval was given for twenty-two more bases, sixteen of them for the USAAF. Some £6.5 million a month was the cost to the Air Ministry of these immense projects and labour was recruited from far and wide – over 50,000, accommodated in special camps, were engaged in this work by May. Some farmers were unhappy as their land was taken from them by compulsory order.

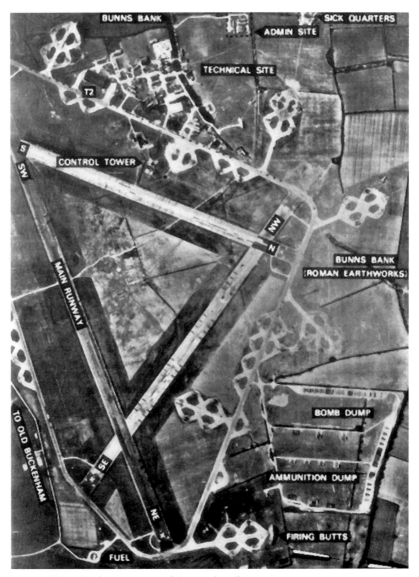

RAF Old Buckenham, near Attleborough, taken in 1946.

An airfield generally would need: a runway 2,000 yards long and 50 yards wide; hangars usually 240 feet long and 115 feet wide; tens of miles of drains; probably two underground fuel stores holding 100,000 gallons of aviation spirit each; and a sewerage plant. The cost of each was supposed to not exceed

£800,000 but frequently did. The work was considerably hurried up with the arrival of American heavy machinery and engineers. The first American bombers in Norfolk were the 319th Bomb Group (Medium) in Shipdham. In October the 44th Bomb Group arrived. The Americans also took over some RAF bases, including Horsham St Faith in Norwich.

Many of the 28,000 Americans who operated from Shipdham were talented artists and the walls were decorated with girls, aircraft and scenes from home. In 2014 an appeal was launched to save these works of art from the ravages of weather and neglect.

At the end of 1942 there were 510 operational airfields in Britain with 157 more in the pipeline.

Before the construction of their designated airfields the US-AAF flew from those operated by the RAF. The first combat operation of the 8th USAAF was from Swanton Morley, just south of Norwich, when American crews flew RAF Douglas Boston light bombers in an attack on airfields in the Low Countries. The first all-American raid was on 17 August when twelve 8th Air Force bombers raided Rouen by day. To the disappointment of the British, no American raids were made against Germany in 1942.

Requisitioning land for the troops: Stanford Battle Area; A tale of mystery and heartbreak

The public was largely impatient for more action but did not know of the massive build up and mobilization of men, women and machines that was going on. Factories were at peak efficiency streaming out planes, trucks, lorries and tanks, and more were coming from America.

More land was needed for Service use and the government authorized the requisition of seven areas of Britain, two of them in East Anglia – 18,000 acres around Thetford and 9,000 behind Orford Ness. In Thetford, 750 people were told to leave their homes and farms – this applied to the villages of West Tofts, Stanford, Langford and Tottington. About 450 people were affected in Orford Ness. There would be no compensation, apart from the cost of the crops, but the land would be given back after the war. The population was very upset but surprisingly compliant – in Thetford, following an address to those affected by Lieutenant-General Sir Kenneth Anderson saying grimly that he was sympathetic but it just

Memorial at Horsham St Faith today.

The King comes to Norfolk.

Troop exercises in a Norfolk village.

had to be done, there was, much to the Lieutenant-General's surprise, a round of applause.

In Theftord a 'Nazi village' was established and important exercises undertaken here in the run-up to D-Day.

The land was never returned. In 2009, in perhaps the absolute ultimate as regards acclimatization for troops about to be posted overseas, an 'Afghan village' was established, at a cost reputed to have been £14 million, complete with Afghan nationals, Gurkhas and wounded soldiers. Machines flooded the village with smells like fetid vegetables, meat that had gone off and raw sewage.

A tragic tale unfolded here. In the late nineteenth century, the daughter of a carpenter in the area had an illegitimate daughter whom she named Lucilla. Her father was never known, even her birth certificate being blank on this point. Lucilla grew up to be a very colourful character, being of blunt no-nonsense nature and very good with a gun. She farmed here and was reluctant to leave in 1942 but was eventually persuaded to leave upon a promise that she could return when hostilities ended. She also received £800 compensation. However, in 1945 she began a fruitless five-year campaign to regain her land, eventually being told by the government that she would never be allowed to return. This broke her heart and, on Remembrance Sunday 1950, she hanged herself. Her faithful dog refused for a long time to let anyone near her body. She was buried in unconsecrated ground on the edge of Tottington church as suicide victims were not allowed to be buried inside church land. In time, however, the boundary of the graveyard was increased and she thus now lies in the confines of the church in which she had worshipped for many years.

Being a protected area, many varieties of wild life in the broadest sense thrive here. The great crested newt, the stone curlew and woodlark have each made a home. Some 600 registered flowering plants, 28 of which are classified as rare, have been identified, as well as over 30 varieties of butterfly and 400 moths. The water systems support the otter – reintroduced in the 1990s – as well as brown trout, dace, eel and pike.

Good news: El Alamein

In November came the welcome news of a major allied victory at El Alamein when General Montgomery struck effectively against the legendary Rommel. It prompted Churchill to say 'This is not the end. It is not even the beginning of the end. But it is, perhaps, the end of the beginning....' In Norfolk, as in the rest of the country, there was definite hope that all may yet be well.

Some Norfolk Soldiers, Sailors and Airmen/ Aircraftwomen and Civilian Dead

John Lansbury James Bales, Able Seaman aboard HMS *Marne*, died when his ship was torpedoed on 12 November 1942. He was 29 years old, the son of George and Ruth Bales of St Germans, Norfolk and husband to Ida Mary of Magdalen, Norfolk. He has no known grave. His brother, Eric George, also died. He is commemorated on Portsmouth Naval Memorial. Additional details: HMS *Marne* was launched on 30 October

British troops at El Alamein.

1940 and suffered great damage just after 2 am when hit by two torpedoes from *U-515* which had just sunk HMS *Hecla*.

Anthony Frederick Barnes, Stoker, 2nd Class C/KX 132331, HM Submarine *P-514*, Royal Navy, was killed on 21 June 1942, aged 20. This submarine, built in America, was travelling from Argentina to St John's Newfoundland when she was rammed and sunk accidentally by a British convoy. Anthony Barnes was the son of Austin and Gracie Barnes of King's Lynn, Norfolk. He is commemorated on Chatham Naval Memorial, Kent.

Jack Aston Bloomfield, Ordinary Seaman C/JX 318967, HMS *Blean*, Royal Navy, died 11 December 1942, aged 19. The *Blean* was on convoy duty off the coast of Algeria when she was torpedoed by *U-443*. Jack Bloomfield was the son of Horace

HMS Marne, *still afloat, being towed into Gibraltar.*

HMS Blean.

HMS Dorsetshire *(rear) and HMS* Cornwall *under attack by the Japanese.*

and Maud Bloomfield of Diss, Norfolk and is commemorated on Chatham Naval Memorial, Kent.

Harold David Clarke, Stoker LT/KX 137278, HMS Trawler *Stella Capella*, Royal Naval Patrol Service, died 19 March 1942, aged 19. HMS *Stella Capella* was torpedoed by *U-701* south of Iceland and sank in less than three minutes. Harold Clarke was the son of John and Ethel Clarke of Sheringham. He has no known grave and is commemorated on Lowestoft Naval Memorial.

(Thomas) Bernard Crowfoot DFC, Pilot Officer (Pilot) 129665 106 Squadron, Royal Air Force Volunteer Reserve, died 15 October 1942, aged 30. He was the son of George and Ellen Crowfoot and husband of Gladys Dorothy Crowfoot of Thetford, Norfolk. He is buried in Rheinberg War Cemetery, Germany.

Phyllis Mary Duffield, Aircraftwoman 2nd Class, Women's Auxiliary Air Force, died on Monday, 2 March 1942. She is commemorated on Runnymede Memorial, Surrey.

Minesweeping.

Distinguished Flying Cross.

The Jarvis family were killed at 41 Patteson Road, Norwich, Norfolk during a 'Baedeker' raid on 27 April 1942. They were Frederick William Jarvis, aged 60; Mrs May Martha Jarvis, aged 56; Miss Dorothy May Jarvis, aged 27 and Miss Beris Mabel Jarvis, aged 25. They all lie in Norwich Cemetery.

Bertie George Noble, Marine CH/23264 HMS *Cornwall*, Royal Marines, died 5 April 1942, aged 38. HMS *Cornwall* and her sister ship HMS *Dorsetshire* became detached from the Eastern Fleet and were unable to defend themselves against fifty Japanese dive bombers. Some 190 crew aboard the *Cornwall* were lost. Bertie Noble, a resident of Diss in Norfolk, was the son of Walter Noble of Paddington, London and is commemorated on Chatham Naval Memorial.

William Phillips, Surgeon Lieutenant, HMS *Niger*, Royal Naval Volunteer Reserve, died 6 July 1942, aged 30. HMS *Niger*, unable to take correct bearings in bad weather, struck a mine in a British-laid minefield. William Phillips was the son of Sidney and Mary Phillips of Overy Staithe, Norfolk. He is commemorated on Chatham Naval Memorial, Kent.

Edward (known as Ralph or Ted) Smith, Lance Corporal 5775718 6th Battalion, Norfolk Regiment, is listed as missing, believed killed, in Yong Peng, Singapore, on 20 January 1942, during the Japanese invasion of Malaya and Singapore. He was 23 years old and the son of Arthur and Florence Smith of Mundesley, Norfolk. He has no known grave and is commemorated on Singapore Memorial, Kranji, Column 48.

Thomas Ellis Stannard, Able Seaman C/J 89853, HMS *Niger*, Royal Navy, died 6 July 1942, aged 37. HMS *Niger* was a Halcyon-Class Minesweeper and was leading a number of Merchantmen home to Britain when she lost her bearings and ran into a British minefield off Iceland. Six of the Merchant ships went down with her (see entry, William Phillips above). Thomas Stannard was the son of Thomas and Caroline Stannard and husband of Kathleen Lucie Stannard of Diss, Norfolk. He is commemorated on the Chatham Naval memorial, Kent.

Margaret Iris Thompson, Wren 10781, HMS *Minos*, Women's Royal Naval Service, died 13 January 1942. There is no concrete evidence to verify the facts but it is likely she died during the attack on Lowestoft Harbour by German Dorniers when her ship was on defence duties. Over seventy were killed during this raid. She was the daughter of George and Isabella Thompson of Holt, Norfolk and is buried in Holt Burial Ground.

George Ernest Weston DFC, Squadron Leader (41885), pilot with 61 Squadron, died Thursday, 1 October 1942, aged 23. He completed over forty missions and the *London Gazette* recorded that he 'displayed outstanding gallantry, skill and determination throughout' the mission for which he was awarded the DFC. He lost his life as the pilot of a Lancaster bomber which crashed upon take off, killing all the crew. His father was originally from Hemblington, Norfolk but later moved to Nelson City, New Zealand.

CHAPTER FIVE

1943

At A Glance: Local and World events

JANUARY

Local

First USAAF raids are launched on Germany – Wilhelmshaven.
First raid on Berlin is made by Mosquitos from RAF Marham.
First Anglo-American weddings take place in Norfolk.

World

Casablanca conference is held between Churchill and Roosevelt.
German offensive in Russia ends. Montgomery enters Tripoli.
Japanese begin evacuation of Guadalcanal.

FEBRUARY

Local

Norfolk celebrates 25th anniversary of Red Army.

World

Bombing raids on industrial targets by RAF and USAAF are
increased. Russian troops capture Kursk, Rostov and Kharkov.

MARCH

Local

Essex Regiment fight in Tunisia. Raid on Great Yarmouth kills
thirteen WRNS.

World

Spring thaw bogs down armies in Russia. Japanese attack Darwin. Record losses are suffered by Allied shipping in Battle of Atlantic.

APRIL

Local

Coastal Belt is designated a 'regulated area'.

World

Battle of U-boats in Atlantic turns in favour of Allies. Eighth Army captures Sousse, Sfax and Enfidaville.

MAY

Local

Low level attacks by Luftwaffe on Norfolk ports leads to heavy loss of life. The American Red Cross Forces Club takes over the Bishop's Palace in Norwich.

World

Tunis and Bizerte are taken by Allies on same day. All Italian and German troops in North Africa surrender. Churchill addresses both Houses of Congress in Washington. Battle of Atlantic ends.

JUNE

Local

Family meetings organized by Red Cross for Japanese PoWs.

World

No Atlantic convoy attacked for first time. King George VI visits Malta.

JULY

Local

Campaign to collect scrap stepped up. Letters received from PoWs in Japanese hands.

World

Allies invade Sicily. USAAF attacks Rome. Allies launch heavy bombing raids on Hamburg and Ruhr. Mussolini is dismissed by King Victor Emmanuel III.

AUGUST

Local

Ninety-one planes are lost by USAAF in East Anglian raids on Peenemunde and Schweinfurt. Town volunteers help gather in the harvest in ideal weather.

B-17F over Schweinfurt, 1943.

WORLD

Mountbatten made Supreme Commander, SE Asia Command. Allies continue heavy bombing of Italy and Germany. Operation Overlord confirmed by Churchill and Roosevelt.

SEPTEMBER

Local

Troops concentrated in Eastern counties to counter invasion.

World

Invasion of Italy begins. US 5th Army lands in Gulf of Salerno to fierce German opposition. Russians recapture Smolensk.

OCTOBER

Local

Norwich School art collection given to city by Russell Colman. Sixty-two Fortresses lost by USAAF on 'Black Thursday'. Siam-Burma Railway completed by PoWS including many men from Norfolk.

World

Italy declares war on Germany. Churchill and Stalin clash on tactics in Arctic. US 5th Army captures Naples. Corsica is liberated.

NOVEMBER

Local

The 5th Essex troops build bridgeheads across Trigno and Sangro rivers in Italy.

World

Heavy night raids on Berlin begin. German troops suffer badly in Russia. Conferences are held involving Churchill, Roosevelt and Chiang Kai-Shek and Churchill, Roosevelt and Stalin.

DECEMBER

Local

Nine Lancasters and four Halifaxes are lost to the RAF on returning to East Anglia in bad weather. D-Day rehearsal in Scotland involves 1st Norfolks and 1st Suffolks. Farmers revolt over prices.

World

Eisenhower is appointed Supreme Commander of Allied invasion with Montgomery in charge of landings. Russian troops are halted by winter conditions in advance. The Pacific Islands War proceeds steadily for US forces.

'Nice chap, no General.' General Montgomery's first impression of General Eisenhower.

Aircraft, airfields and airmen

Aircraft, airfields and airmen dominated East Anglia to such an extent as 1943 progressed that many refer to the region at the time as the largest flight deck the world has ever seen (if we take the whole of Britain as the aircraft carrier). The Empire

Some American airmen were fine artists and today a scheme is underway to save some of the murals that were painted on the base walls before neglect and weather irreparably ruin them: this painting is at Shipdham.

A USAAF Liberator flying over the Norfolk village of Hempnall.

B-17G BO, 'Wee Willie' takes a direct hit on her 128th mission. Only the pilot, Lieutenant Robert E. Fuller, survived.

Affectionate cartoon showing the strengths in defence and attack of the Fortress.

Unusual close-up photograph of a Martin B-26 Marauder.

and Commonwealth came, too – it is estimated that even at the start of the year, 37 per cent of Bomber Command pilots were from New Zealand, Canada and Australia. Then came the Americans, up from about 20,000 at the start of the war to 185,000 by the end of 1943. To accommodate them, the RAF gave up some of its airfields including Horsham St Faiths in Norwich.

The construction of new airfields for both the RAF and USAAF was given top priority, the workers recruited from anywhere and everywhere and paid unheard of wages, with the whole project provided with a £615 million budget. The US Army Engineer Battalions also built many including Great Saling, Eye and Great Dunmow.

New airfields and those of the RAF assigned to the Eighth Army Air Force in 1943 were: Framlingham, Earls Colne, Andrewsfield (May); Boxted, Chipping Ongar, Great Dunmow, Ridgewell, Thorpe Abbots, Snetterton Heath, Knettishall, Great Ashfield (June); Bodney, Steeple Morden, Halesworth (July); Metfield and Wendling (August); East Wretham, Martlesham Heath (August); Tibenham and Deenethorpe, Seething, Raydon, Leiston (November); Old Buckenham (December). To each of the airfields the Eighth Army Air Force assigned one bomb group of thirty-two to thirty-six bombers. Of the three

American recruitment poster featuring a Marauder.

divisions, one was for a time headquartered at Old Catton and then Horsham St Faiths in Norwich before moving quite close by to Ketteringham Hall.

The Americans also had three fighter wings in East Anglia flying from twelve airfields in Norfolk, Suffolk, Essex and Cambridgeshire.

The American planes were a source of fascination to local people, especially schoolboys: the Boeing B-17, known as the 'Flying Fortress' (which had a fair few technical problems before the highly sophisticated B-17G took to the air in September); the B-24 Liberators and the B-26 Marauders. The RAF had the new Mitchell bombers, the Lancasters, Stirlings and Halifaxes. These planes were almost constantly in the skies over Norfolk to the chagrin of some, including local vicars who found their sermons sometimes drowned out by the screech, thunder and roar of engines. One or two vicars took to the press to ask if such continuous flights were *really* necessary.

B-17 Flying Fortresses over Europe.

The year begins with Churchill unhappy

'War is mainly a catalogue of blunders.'

Winston Churchill

Churchill and Roosevelt met at Casablanca in mid-January 1943 and Churchill made it clear to the commander of the Eighth, Brigadier-General Ira Eaker, that he was not happy: with 20,000 US men and 500 machines in East Anglia, not one bomb had so far been dropped on Germany. Almost immediately, on 27 January, fifty-three Flying Fortresses attacked the naval base at Wilhelmshaven and this signalled the beginning of a joint non-stop assault by British and American forces. All was not in harmony, however, as the British had sought to harm the morale of German workers

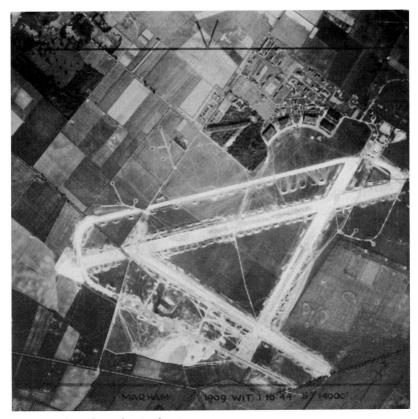

RAF Marham from the air showing new concrete runways.

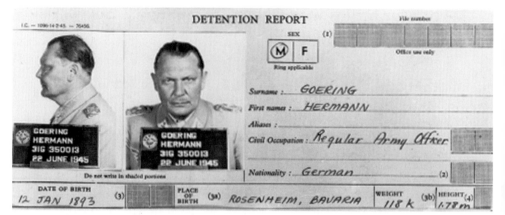

American Mugshots of Goering after capture.

by direct attacks while the Americans believed in high-level bombing – this divergence in attitude continued in 1943.

The conference led to common sustained assault on the U-boats – in 1942 1,160 Allied vessels had been sunk and by January 1943 the number of U-boats had more than doubled to 212. On 27 January, the 93rd Bomb Group at Hardwick joined in a massive attack – sixty-four aircraft – on U-boat pens at Atlantic ports and construction yards at Vegesack, this raid including Fortresses from Shipden in Norfolk.

First attack on Berlin comes from RAF Marham; Saturation bombing inhumane?

Three Mosquitos of RAF Bomber Command, flying from Marham in Norfolk, were the first to attack Berlin – this was on 30 January, ten years to the day that Hitler had been sworn in as Chancellor of Germany. They were over Berlin at 11.00 am, dropped their bombs and returned to Norfolk safely. This was a propaganda coup also as Goering was forced to postpone for an hour a speech he planned to deliver at this time. Unfortunately, the day of triumph for Marham was marred when another attack by three Mosquitos at 4.00 pm was met by the Luftwaffe and one plane was lost. Berlin suffered a further huge assault on 3 March.

RAF Venturas and US Fortresses attacked Brest and Dunkirk on 1 March and the raids continued, aimed principally on the U-boat bases. In the first five months of the year 20,000 tons of high explosives and incendiaries were dropped. Despite this, it was later claimed, after the war, that not a single U-boat was hampered by these attacks, and it was only by July that more Allied ships were being produced than sunk.

The British public were ambivalent to the heavy bombing raids and some MPs thought them inhumane and even

Sir Arthur Harris.

487 Squadron NCOs at RAF Methwold in front of a Lockheed Ventura, early 1943.

The Mohne Dam after breaching.

indefensible. However, Air Chief Marshal Sir Arthur Harris planned saturation bombing in three phases, beginning in March with the 'Battle of the Ruhr', then summer saw the 'Battle of Hamburg' and in November came the 'Battle of Berlin'. Historians have maintained that these attacks were nothing like as successful as the media of the time asserted – in fact, German armament production grew at an alarming pace in 1943 and losses, for both the RAF and the Americans on their daylight raids, were grievous. Norfolk residents saw for themselves on a daily basis the armadas go out and the far fewer numbers of damaged planes limping home. Everyone was on permanent standby to help out. In one instance, a farm hand had just gone to bed when he heard and felt the tremors of a crash. He rushed out in the darkness to find a blazing German bomber with the four surviving crew in a state of disorientation and shock. Pretending in the gloom to have a gun, he pointed his hand at the men who immediately surrendered. In another incident, a lone German pilot tried to surrender at the nearest building he could find which happened to be a pub. The landlord had been having trouble with some of his regulars that evening and thought it was one of them coming back. He opened his bedroom window and yelled 'Go away!' The pilot apparently persisted and found another house at which to give himself up.

Between March and July the Ruhr was under continuous attack by the Allies. In May two of Germany's greatest dams – the Mohne and Eder – were destroyed. May also saw a disastrous mission from Methwold in Norfolk when a dozen Venturas set out for the steelworks at Ijmuiden in Holland. Their escort fighters were forced to return home because of a lack of fuel and eleven were downed.

Two great escapes

In 2015, a remarkable find was made off Blakeney, Norfolk – the remains of a USAAF B-17 Flying Fortress which took off with nine men on board. The story was corroborated by Lieutenant Colonel John Gorse, the nephew of the bomber's 19-year-old co-pilot, 2nd Lieutenant Norville Gorse who survived the crash. The bomber was flying on 13 May 1943 as part of a mission to St Omer in France when a machine gun went off without warning, hitting two crew members and shooting off the right stabilizer. Captain Derrol Rogers and Norville Gorse managed to control the plane for two hours, allowing seven crew to jettison safely and dumping the bombs in the Wash. The Captain told Norville Gorse to jump before ditching the plane in the sea. Lieutenant Gorse was picked up an hour later by a rescue boat and survived but Captain Rogers died of exposure.

Lieutenant Gorse was at the controls of another Fortress, Dallas Rebel, on 28 July when German fighters forced the plane to ditch along with five men – three of whom had been on the flight of 13 May – who together spent several days afloat, at one time being circled by a hungry shark which after one 'circle' decided to seek prey elsewhere. The men were rescued by the Germans. Neville Gorse spent the remainder of the war in prisoner-of-war camps, beginning with the infamous Stalag LUFT III which was featured in the iconic 1963 film *The Great Escape* starring Steve McQueen, James Garner and Richard Attenborough. He died in 2003.

USAAF's heavy losses; Flying bombs

Handsome Young Airman

Oh, a handsome young airman lay dying
Surrounded by wreckage he lay
And the mechanics who stood all around him
Swear these are the words he did say, did say.

Take the cylinders out of my kidneys
Connecting rods out of my brain
From the small of my back take the crankshaft
Assemble Pratt Whitney again, again

Now whenever you're flying the 'Big B's'
Or airplanes of similar ilk,
Never forget the old ripcord
And always resort to the silk, the silk.

Oh the Big 'B's' a mighty fine airplane
Constructed of rivets and tin
It has a top speed of 150
The ship with the headwind built in, built in.

I never should have joined the Air Corps
Mother, dear Mother knew best
For now I lay here in the wreckage
Pratt Whitney all over my chest, my chest.

Anonymous

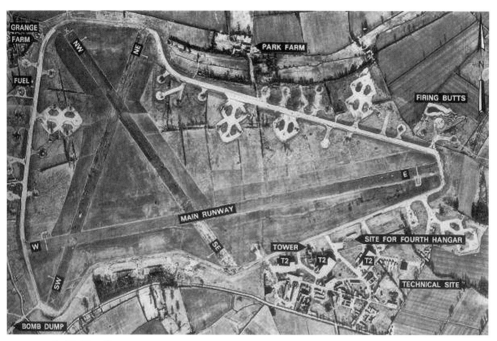

RAF Shipdham.

B-17F radar bombing over Bremen, 1943.

No. 431

BURNHAMS Market & Norton

Wings for Victory Week—

May 29 - June 5
1943

Souvenir
Programme

Price 3D.

Fund raising under various guises was unrelenting.

The USAAF continued to mount large assaults of up to 200 planes at a time but the losses were sapping morale – by mid-June 42 planes and over 300 crew had been lost. However, raids continued between July and November – for instance, between those dates, there were thirty-three RAF, USAAF and combined attacks on the Hamburg region. Some of the latest Liberators, and other aircraft, were also sent from Norfolk airfields, including Shipdham, to attack targets in Africa and Italy at this time. A major assault was made by the Eighth Army Air Force on 17 August when 300 planes bombed the Messerschmitt factory at Regensburg and a ball-bearing factory at Schweinfurt with the loss of sixty. The following night saw 600 bombers leave East Anglia for the experimental station at Peenemunde in the Baltic – forty were shot down and fifteen crashed coming home.

The raids on Berlin became more frequent in the summer. On 23 August 700 British bombers dropped 1,700 tons of bombs on the Nazi capital with the loss of 123 planes. Air Chief Marshal Harris persisted, despite criticism and horror from many quarters, in his campaign. The 563rd squadron at Knettishall in Essex was wiped out when 45 of their planes were shot down attacking Stuttgart on 6 September. General Eaker sent 400 bombers to attack Bremen on 8 October and thirty-one were lost. On 10 October sixteen bomb groups attacked Munster against a well-prepared enemy who destroyed thirty Fortresses.

A 15-inch coastal defence gun in Singapore.

The date 14 October was 'Black Thursday' when the Eighth Air Force sent out 291 Fortresses on various missions – only thirty came back undamaged. In this one week the USAAF lost 148 aircraft. On 23/4/5 October raids on Berlin saw 5,000 tons of bombs dropped.

Reports of base life at this time often inevitably make tragic reading – officers at debriefings simply in tears not knowing what to say; bases akin to morgues; breakfast where yesterday there were dozens of pilots laughing and joking and today just a few unable to eat anything. Ridgewell was one such after the attacks of 17 August when 100 men had been lost. It was rebuilt, however, and there is a legendary footnote. On 2 December two of the missing men walked into the base: they had baled out, evaded capture and trekked home out of Germany, across France aided by the Resistance, and into England, existing all the while on root vegetables.

In autumn came news of a new weapon being developed by eighty-eight launching sites across the Continent – a pilot-less 'flying bomb'. There were fears not only for the future of London but of the planned invasion of Europe should these new weapons be allowed to develop. From the end of November fighter-bombers of the RAF 2nd Tactical Air Force, aided by US Fortresses and Liberators, launched raids on these bases and up to fifty more that reconnaissance indicated were in preparation. Industrial targets continued to be bombed also over the Christmas and New Year period.

Singapore, the Royal Norfolks and the 'Railway of Death'

'Singapore could only be taken after a siege by an army of at least 50,000 men. It is not considered possible that the Japanese would embark on such a mad enterprise.'

Winston Churchill

'My attack on Singapore was a bluff, a bluff that worked... I was very frightened that all the time the British would discover our numerical weakness and lack of supplies and force me into disastrous street fighting.'

General Yamashita

When Singapore surrendered, many men from East Anglia became prisoners of war. They were from three battalions of the Royal Norfolk Regiment, the 4th, 5th and 6th, two battalions of the Suffolk Regiment, the 4th and 5th, and the 1st and 2nd battalions of the Cambridgeshire Regiment. Conditions on Singapore Island were harsh and the poor diet resulted in various health problems – dysentery, ulcers, malaria and eye problems amongst many. In this period, two British soldiers who tried to escape were shot. Families in Norfolk received very little information about the fate of their loved ones, the first lists of prisoners arriving only in March 1943 and these itemized barely one in ten of the missing.

Late in 1942 and early in 1943 the men were split up, and sent to Thailand, Burma, Indonesia, Formosa (now Taiwan), the Philippines and Japan. Some 61,000 were sent to build the railway that was to link Bangkok and Moulmein in Burma, later known as the 'Railway of Death'. The Royal Norfolks left Singapore in March by train – 550 in total from the 5th and 6th battalions. They were packed into red hot wagons that burnt their flesh when touching the sides and were fed just rice. Their base camp on arrival was at Chungkai, 100 miles west of Bangkok, where there were altogether about 6,000 British prisoners.

Most officers, contrary to the Geneva Convention, were forced to work. However, discipline was partly maintained and the prisoners divided into work battalions – for instance, the 4th Suffolks and the 4th Royal Norfolks were allocated to the No 8 Work Battalion, and the 5th Royal Norfolks to the No 16 Work Battalion. The battalions were sent forward, leap-frogging each other, clearing virgin forest and mountain track with no machinery. The daily diet was twenty ounces of rice, twenty ounces of vegetables, under four ounces of meat, and a little salt, sugar and tea. The climate was searing, conditions in the camps insanitary and as many as half the men were often sick – of cholera, beri-beri, malaria, amoebic dysentery, diphtheria and malnutrition – at the same time. There was no mercy or respite for the sick and many East Anglians died from unimaginable cruelty.

Writing materials were forbidden but two diaries – from Captain R.G. de Quincy and Dr Robert Hardie – were written,

Bridge over the River Kwai by Leo Rawlings, 1943.

hidden and survive. Dr Hardie's diary has been published in full by the Imperial War Museum and depicts beatings, kickings, face spitting and any humiliation that the Japanese and Korean guards could think of. Often beatings were from the 'pickle stick' which was a bamboo cane about two inches in diameter and four feet long – some men, too sick to move, were beaten to death.

Many men were subsequently marched for nine days to Takanun where conditions were appalling and cholera broke out: thirty-five men died. East Anglian men were here in Nos 5, 8 and 16 battalions.

At home, in June, there were meetings where the British Red Cross gave what little information they had about these men to relatives. One was in Cambridge, one in Norwich (Stuart and Suckling Halls) and one in the Town Hall at King's Lynn. All were burst to overflowing. It was confirmed at this time that Norfolk had more prisoners of war in the Far East than any

AUSTRALIAN WAR MEMORIAL   P00761.011

Starving Australian and Dutch PoWS working on the railway.

other county. The Japanese forbade parcels but postcards began to arrive and by July many families received news – although always saying variations of the same thing, that the sender was in good health and was well treated – of their menfolk.

According to the Commonwealth War Graves Commission, some 13,000 soldiers died during the construction of the railway; this was alongside 80,000 to 100,000 civilians, mainly forced labour from the Dutch East Indies, Burma, Siam and Malaya.*

*In 1952, the French novelist, Pierre Boulle, wrote *Le Pont de la Riviere Kwai*. It is fictional, a story depicting the experiences of British prisoners building the bridge over the Mae Klong (there is no actual Bridge over the River Kwai). Boulle had been a prisoner of war in Thailand. The book won the Prix Saint-Beuve in 1952. A famous film directed by David Lean, *The Bridge over the River Kwai*, won the Academy Award for Best Picture in 1957. After the success of the film the Thais faced a problem as large numbers of tourists came to see the bridge, which did not actually exist. The problem was solved by renaming the Mae Klong river the Kwae Yai for several miles – the bridge built by the prisoners being on this stretch.

Louis Mountbatten, 1st Earl Mountbatten of Burma.

The railway was opened at the end of October, and the Allies started to bomb it. The men from Norfolk were split up and sent all over the Pacific, some dying as the prisoner ships were torpedoed.

Admiral Lord Louis Mountbatten was made Supreme Commander in August and his forces, stationed at Ahmadnagar in India, included the men of the 2nd battalion, the Royal Norfolks. The Allies and the increasingly confident Americans were on the ascendancy as the year came to an end. Despite inevitable horrors ahead, the war in the Pacific could only end in one way now.

Meanwhile, thousands of Norfolk families waited for news: at the end of 1943, of the 52,000 men in Asia, the Red Cross had names of only 30,000. Of the others, nothing had been heard for two years.

Other fronts on which troops from East Anglia were fighting

> *'Before Alamein, we had no victories. After Alamein, we had no defeats.'*
>
> Winston Churchill

El Alamein had rounded off 1942 on a victorious note and a full-length film shot by the Army and RAF Production

General Sir Harold Alexander.

Units played to packed cinemas in spring 1943. In January
Montgomery further pushed Rommel back and crossed into
Tunisia in February. The 7th Cambridgeshires had now become
the 142nd Regiment of the Royal Armoured Corps. They landed
at Algiers in February. The Regiment was joined by the 1st/4th
Battalion, Essex Regiment. On 7 May, following an attack by
the Essex Regiment which cleared the ground, aided by the
142nd Regiment, the 11th Hussars entered and occupied Tunis;
50,000 prisoners were taken. General Alexander, in command
of all Allied land forces was able to message Churchill: 'All
enemy resistance has ceased. We are masters of the North

General Bernard Montgomery.

African shores', and the men from Cambridgeshire took part in a victory parade in Tunis on 20 May.

There followed the invasion of Sicily, Mussolini's resignation and, on 8 September, Italy's unconditional surrender. The 1st/5th Essex thereafter fought a bitter battle against the occupying Germans and lost 13 officers and 266 men. Late in September the 30th Battalion of the Royal Norfolks and the 31st Battalion of the Cambridgeshires arrived. The Royal Norfolks spent the first week-and-a-half guarding prisoners but then moved on to Syracuse. Remarkably they then became a 'phantom' division, the 152nd Brigade with fictitious officers, brigadiers and adjutants, the purpose of which was to confuse the enemy and, as such, they did various jobs around Syracuse for the rest of the year.

The other front that was of consuming interest to people at home was the battle for Russia. The Russians were now on the offensive and there followed a mania for everything Russian in East Anglia. Around Norfolk, in practically every town and village, the 25th anniversary of the creation of the Red Army was celebrated by processions in the streets. All was not quite as rosy for the Russians as the newspapers and radio maintained and it was not until Christmas Eve that a new Russian offensive near Kiev broke through the German lines and troops prepared to enter Poland. But one of the chief Christmas presents this year was *War and Peace* or any other Tolstoy novel, if you could find a shop that had not sold out.

On Boxing Day came the incredible news that the *Scharnhorst*, the German navy's pride and joy, had been sunk by the Royal Navy off Norway. And on the last day of the year, 3,000 planes from bases in Norfolk and elsewhere raided targets in Europe, whilst the Russians were reported to have routed twenty-two German divisions.

Strangers in Norfolk

In 1565 Norwich had invited Protestant refugees from the Spanish Netherlands to live in the city to boost the textile industry. Thirty master weavers and their families came over and then many more, eventually accounting for a third of the city's population. Today, the word 'strangers' is a common one in Norwich on buildings, coffee shops, food take-aways, streets and pubs. It simply means 'people from other places'. Norwich has for hundreds of years, then, benefited from the skills of people from other lands.

Men of the Essex Regiment firing 3-inch mortars, Orford, December 1942.

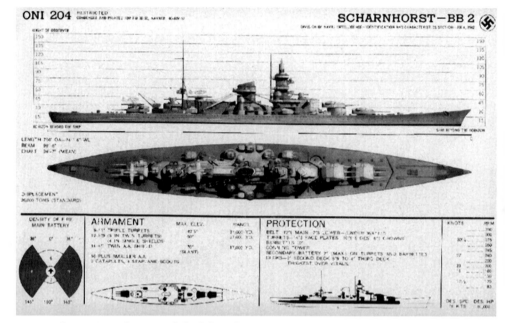

Recognition drawing of the Scharnhorst.

This is not the case in Norfolk as a whole. From the sixteenth century until the Great War it has been in many ways a land apart. Many people did not travel out of their village or town for the whole of their lives and, as the county is not on the way to anywhere else, it saw very few visitors or passers-by. By 1943 this situation had changed permanently out of all recognition.

In the Great War had come servicemen from all over Britain, not only to Norwich but to defend the 'critical coastline' of Norfolk – Hunstanton, Cromer, Sheringham, and Great Yarmouth – which was seen as a highly likely place for an invasion. Between the wars, the often sparsely populated county had largely reverted to its isolation. In 1939 citizens of the Commonwealth arrived, especially from Canada, Australia and New Zealand, as well as individual Americans wanting to fight for the Allies. Then came Poles, Norwegians, Dutch, Free French and Czechs. Finally, as highlighted already, tens of thousands of Americans travelled to Norfolk who, as well as fighting and giving their lives alongside British flyers in their thousands, also brought chocolate, nylons, dancing and a sprinkling of Hollywood stardust to Norfolk towns and villages.

According to the Mass Observation organization, 48 per cent of Norfolk people were pro-American and those of influence in the county tried to increase friendly feelings. The Bishop of Norwich gave up his Bishop's Palace to the American Red Cross (although retaining sole use of his library). Anglo-American Service Clubs proliferated and garden parties, sports competitions and outings of all kinds were organized. Friendships and some marriages resulted – Norwich at the end of 1943 witnessed the first marriage of an Englishman to a member of the US forces, that of Mr Thomas Thompson, grandson of one-time MP for Great Yarmouth, Sir Arthur Harbord, to Sergeant Jane Freytag of the American WAC. In villages large and small there developed a 'Mother for a Day' scheme where a local woman would take a GI out for lunch and tea.

The authorities saw a colour problem not shared by the general public as a whole. Some American GIs were black but by now 10,000 West Indians were already in the RAF as well. The War Office issued guidance to the effect that races should not fraternize but at the same time said they would not cooperate in a policy of segregation; and 'zoning' was practised by both the locals and Americans, which was where individual public houses were reserved for the sole use of one racial group or another.

There were also Italian prisoners of war – by the end of the year 52,000 of them housed in camps mainly but some also permitted to live in the farms on which they predominantly worked. Many of them were popular with the locals, although the authorities banned absolutely any fraternization which resulted in some strangely comic court cases where local people – girls mostly – had maybe exchanged a note or chatted too long.

There has been a Jewish community in Norwich since 1066 and they have been successful and influential. It is quite possible that the Anglican Cathedral only managed to be built under the direction of Herbert de Losinga because the Jewish people lent money. More recently, the Jewish firm of Haldinstein, now part of Bally, was responsible for thousands of pairs of army boots,

Hunstanton's famous layered cliff showing the wreck of the trawler Sheraton
which served in both wars but was wrecked by a storm soon afterwards. (photo:
Daniel Tink)

supreme in quality and much envied by the Germans, during the Great War: So, in Norwich, the Jewish community had long been influential but it was also very small in number. Despite there being about 450,000 Jews in England in 1939, many of whom were escaping the Nazis, the number in Norwich probably did not exceed 150. The Synagogue in St Faith Lane was destroyed by bombs in 1942 and only rebuilt permanently in 1968.

Poland and Norfolk

There are many people in Norwich and Norfolk today with a Polish background and a dedicated memorial in the Roman Catholic Cathedral of St John the Baptist celebrates this fact. Many Poles fled their homeland in 1939 and subsequently found their way to England, notably Norfolk among other counties. Some joined the RAF and were stationed at East Anglian bases and this includes the 307 Squadron at Coltishall and Horsham St Faiths. Many stayed on, some getting married and taking British nationality.

The actions of the British government are controversial, particularly in withdrawing recognition of the London-based Polish government-in-exile in 1945 at Stalin's request. Thereafter around 200 Polish resettlement camps were opened using former army barracks, hospitals, military hospitals and former RAF bases and these acted as temporary homes to about 125,000 people which almost doubled in the next few years as people feared for their lives if they returned to Poland. Many Poles also sought a home in other counties in Britain and countries including the USA, Canada, Australia and New Zealand.

There were eight camps around Thetford – at Weeting Hall, Bodney Airfield (2), Shakers Wood, London Road, Dixon East Camp, the Quadrilateral Camp and Riddlesworth Hall School. The last camp was closed in 1969.

There is a lively Polish presence in Norfolk nowadays and a Polish/Norfolk heritage group. In June 2017 the Wianki Celebration – pre-Christian Polish mid-summer festival celebrating the wearing of wreaths – was held for the first time.

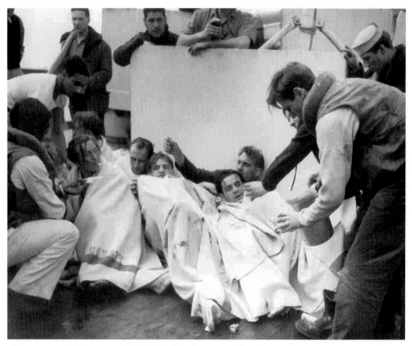

Survivors of submarine U-175 *after being sunk, 17 April 1943.*

Many memorial services are held each year, including in 2017, a service led by Reverend Canon Bob Baker, Rector of Thetford, in East Wretham where fourteen aircrew are buried, twelve of them Czechs and two Poles.

Further information is available using the following internet link – www.norfolkpolishheritagegroup.org

Norfolk coastal towns; Restrictions on civilians

Norfolk coastal towns, especially Great Yarmouth, buzzed with activity as ships went out to protect convoys and lay mines. They also continued to be attacked, often by 'lone' hit-and-run bombers, although not as intensely as in 1942.

London was the focal point for the huge collection of forty or fifty ships – the biggest convoy system in the world – that went up and down the East Coast, often bringing coal or going back to get it from the north-east ports. The government wanted a two-year supply in advance of the D-Day landings so that the ships could then be useful in other ways. The convoys progressed in two parallel lines, 7 miles long. In January 1943 the Nore Command Escort Force consisted of twenty-four destroyers and seven corvettes. The German E-boats were based 90 miles away at Ijmuiden.

Only two ships were lost in the first five months of 1943. A big battle commenced off Cromer on 6 October when twenty-eight boats from Ijmuiden attacked a convoy: two enemy vessels were lost to just one British trawler. On 24 October thirty E-boats attacked another convoy, losing four ships to the Royal Navy's none.

In addition, there were sixty minesweepers based at Great Yarmouth responsible for the coast from Sheringham to Lowestoft. Great Yarmouth also had fifteen motor torpedo boats, twenty motor gunboats and twelve motor launches. Some minesweepers played a vital role in extended convoy operations, for example, to enable ships with armaments to reach Russia after it had been attacked by Germany. One story emerged in the local press in 2014 about an Arctic Star Medal posthumously awarded to Albert Tungate who was once a trainee chemist in Wells. He worked on this perilous route, when he was in his fifties, in temperatures of -50C at times. He had also sailed during the Great War. He died in 1977 aged 83 and the medal was applied for

A WRNS rating in the war.

German Schnellboot S204 *raising the white flag and surrendering to HMS* Beehive, *3 May 1945.*

by his son. In the same year, another to receive this honour, in person from Commander Igor Elkin, the Russian Naval Attache, was 89-year-old Sam Bouch of Gorleston.

Much of the population had evacuated the east-coast ports which became towns run entirely by the Royal Navy, swarming with dedicated staff, including WRNS, who worked all hours. The boats were made of wood and a scent of mahogany hung in the air around the workshops.

There were some skirmishes off the coast with the motor boats engaging E-boats. In one, on 14 April, the legendary senior officer of the 8th MGB Flotilla, Lieutenant-Commander Robert Hichens, DSO, DSC and veteran of 148 actions, was killed by a chance shot. There were some successes for the patrols off the coast off Ijmuiden such as at the end of April when one, under the command of Lieutenant Dickens, sank a tug of 107 tons.

From April the coastal belt, to a depth of 10 miles, was declared a 'regulated area' and civilians warned that they may simply be turned away with no reason given. From October, however, the ban on living in some places on the coast was lifted – to include Hunstanton, Sheringham, Cromer, Mundesley and Caister.

Bombings

The town most targeted by Germany continued to be Great Yarmouth: during the whole of 1943 there were 217 'alerts' during which 72 people were killed and 124 injured. The bombings included the destruction of a WRNS hostel on 18 March, when thirteen girls were killed. The new Focke-Wulf FW.190 fighter-bombers appeared on 7 May, flying very low. Twenty-eight of the same planes returned four days later, killing forty-nine and

Focke-Wulf Fw190.

injuring forty-one in just a few minutes. Raids decreased during the summer and autumn.

Attempts, continuous but largely ineffective, continued to be made to bomb East Anglian airfields. Increased pressure was placed on the lifeboat crews and the RAF air-rescue units as crew from both sides ditched into the sea off Norfolk; theoretically at least if all went according to the training manual, the British flyers had the ability now to use fluorescein to colour the sea yellow-green after they ditched and they were equipped with yellow life jackets.

Food for the troops; American, British, German and Russian

'An army marches on its stomach.'

Napoleon

During the Great War, at least in the very beginning, many Norfolk men had signed up for an adventure, living in tents, subsequently with a chance for glory and to give the Hun a bloody nose and also for another reason – the food. The daily calorific intake of a soldier was far in excess of a man working on the land or in one of the Norwich shoe factories, to take just two of the main areas of employment at the time. A soldier consumed up to 4,000 calories a day and the food was often so rich that many grew constipated and chubby.

By 1939, experts on nutrition and cooking had been to work. **The Americans** came up with the following categories of rations:

A-ration: This was the Garrison ration prepared where a food kitchen or dining hall offered the facilities. It was fresh or frozen food, usually of cheapish ingredients – potatoes, eggs, economy cuts of meat, hot dogs, vegetables, pies and puddings. It was the most popular.

B-ration: A Field ration utilizing packaged and canned foods and none that needed refrigeration.

C-ration: This was an Individual ration: a canned pre-cooked ready meal. Varieties included meat and beans, meat and potato hash and meat and vegetable stew for dinners or chopped ham, egg and potato for breakfast. Also bread or crackers, instant coffee and sugar, nine cigarettes, matches, water purification tablets, chewing gum and toilet paper. Each meal was about 2,000 calories.

K-ration: This was an Individual ration also, but for attack troops such as paratroopers. This meal was under 2,000 calories consisting of more sweets than 'C-ration': and four cigarettes.

D-ration: An Emergency ration of high calorific content but limited nutritional value – sweets, bars of chocolate, biscuits etc.

The British also ate the American rations often on joint operations or on many occasions when special drops were made in the field. However, by 1944, a common 24-hour ration would be one of several versions – the meat would vary – such as the following: 1 tin of Ham/Chicken/Beef/Steak and kidney/ Luncheon meat/Red Salmon or other, 2 packets of Meat Broth, 1 Pack of Oatmeal, 1 bar of chocolate, 1 pack of biscuits, 1 packet of sweets, 2 tea blocks – combination of tea, milk and sugar, 1 packet of sweet biscuits, 2 packs of chewing gum, 2 packs of sugar tablets. Also supplied would be a tin opener and menu sheet, pack of matches and toilet paper. Each man would also have a 'Tommy Cooker' which was little more than a tin heated with hexamine tablets (originally perfected by Germany in 1939).

The German army issued rations similar to American C and K types. However, Hitler ordered that, as far as possible, men should eat solely from the country of occupation and not rely on supplies. This was also designed to force Russia into starvation and submission. In many places, the men ate very well, reports from veterans mentioning field bakeries, food 'delivery' to the trenches and beer. This was not the case as the war progressed or on the Eastern Front. Troops and the Luftwaffe were increasingly issued with amphetamines which, among other effects, suppressed appetite.

Staples of the **Red Army** included:

- Kasha: a buckwheat porridge: simmered and sometimes mixed with meat.
- Okroshka: a soup eaten cold and made of vegetables and any left-over meat.
- Kvass: fermented black bread and very popular.
- Tyurya: Okroshka plus black bread and Kvass.
- Vodka: 100 grams a day.
- Tobacco: 20 grams a day or, for non-smokers, extra chocolate/sweets.

The Russians also received huge quantities of spam from the Americans. This pink food could be eaten cold, made into sandwiches, chopped, fried, baked or put into stews. One of many names (some of them rude) was 'Roosevelt Sausage'. A poem of the time bears witness to its importance:

Now Jackson had his acorns

And Grant his precious rye;

Teddy had his poisoned beef —

Worse you couldn't buy.

The doughboy had his hardtack

Without the navy's jam,

But armies on their stomachs move —

And this one moves on Spam.

Anonymous

Nikita Krushchev wrote in his autobiography, 'Without Spam, we wouldn't have been able to feed our army.'

At home, too, Spam was a vital food. Margaret Thatcher, the future British Prime Minister, recalled how, as a girl in 1943 Britain, a tin would be produced for Sunday afternoon tea. It would be served with salad and followed by tinned peaches.

Upping the game

During 1943, the government demanded the maximum in everything: food production – enough to feed the population for six-and-a-half-days a week, which resulted in village greens being dug up to grow potatoes, the King's private golf course being given over to rye and oats, and the outskirts of Norfolk's airfields starting to produce cabbages; fighting men – the army wanted 250,000 more; Women's Land Army workers – the number stood at over 51,000 in the spring and 1,000 girls were joining every week; more women in every type of job – already nine out of ten unmarried, and eight out of ten married, women were helping the war effort; boys – by October all boys of sixteen had to register at the Ministry of Labour; and fire officers – all men aged between eighteen and sixty-three were now liable for service.

The Women's Land Army was highly organized and supplies were not to be sniffed at: on joining, each girl was supplied with two green jerseys, two pairs of breeches, two overall coats, two pairs of dungarees, six pairs of stockings, three shirts, one pair of ankle boots, one pair of shoes, one pair of gun boots, one hat, one overcoat with shoulder titles, one oilskin or mackintosh, two towels, one oil skin sou'wester, a green armlet and a metal badge: after every six months and again after two years she received special cloth badges culminating after four years with one in scarlet. They also had their own poem:

BACK TO THE LAND

Back to the Land, we must all lend a hand,

To the farms and fields we must go.

There's a job to be done,

Though we can't fire a gun,

We can still do our bit with the hoe.

When your muscles are strong

You will soon get along,

And you'll think that a country life's grand.

We're all needed now,

We must all speed the plough,

So come with us – Back to the Land.

Meanwhile, rations were further reduced – cheese, for example, was restricted to six ounces (previously eight) per person per week and everyone was allowed just one egg a week. Children at school were able to rely on school meals for basic nutrition in some cases only, Norfolk being the worst East Anglian county in this respect with only 19 per cent of elementary pupils benefitting. The Ministry of Food introduced a new 'wonder food' – potato powder, which Lord Woolton proclaimed

Scouts in Norfolk collecting paper.

A toy car, pram, bedstead, bicycle and all manner of scrap for the war effort.

produced mashed potato identical to that produced in the normal manner. Oranges were considered a great prize.

Along with collecting salvage of every kind, a Wings for Victory campaign was launched in the summer of 1943 and in almost every case original targets were exceeded. Norwich raised £1,456,363 and Great Yarmouth, which had more cause than most to be thankful to the RAF, £385,000.

There were many problems. The rumour mill never really ceased – there was always someone with stories of German commandos that had landed in somewhere-or-other and were taking the locals prisoner. A great many Norfolk families were living below the poverty line which was £3 12s 7d a week and there was severe overcrowding, especially with the need to accommodate evacuees both from Norfolk's own coastal belt and London. Children many times ran amok without their fathers but one antidote to this was the Scout movement which increased in numbers: scouts were given work, such as patrolling and collecting clothes, metal and rags, of genuine help to the war effort. In contrast to the Great War, cases of people being taken to court for drunkenness were relatively rare, the result in some places of there simply being no beer.

The autumn saw the return of some men who had been held prisoner in German camps, nine to King's Lynn and six to Norwich – one was able to bring news that there were a further 200 East Anglian prisoners in his camp – Stalag 8b. PoW Associations were formed all over the eastern counties.

Sexual matters

There were now hundreds of thousands of men in East Anglia who were away from home – Americans, Italian prisoners and others. At the same time many resident menfolk were fighting overseas.

The American forces were accused of either 'trying it on' with local girls and women or simply importing train loads of women from London, all expenses paid. They were known as 'shack rats'.

Illegitimate births and venereal disease were on the increase. In 1939 there had been 78 recorded illegitimate births in Norwich and this increased by about 100 every year to a peak of 414 in 1945. Figures are unreliable as not all cases were reported, due to the perceived shame or medical ignorance, but possibly 1,000 cases of venereal disease in Norwich were being treated as the war came to an end – numbers of men and women being about the same. Norfolk was very conservative in attitude with the result that people in polite society wanted neither to discuss nor attend to the matter. The Bishop of Norwich was, however, one who raised the subject, and advocated stronger Christian convictions and an open, caring atmosphere for those who found themselves in trouble. A home for unmarried mothers and others at risk was funded in the city and the Chief Constable of Norwich, Mr J.H. Dain, spearheaded a campaign to stop alcohol being supplied to young persons under eighteen.

The *Eastern Daily Press* reported that young women were not safe to walk in some parts of Norfolk towns and villages after dark, especially when the pubs emptied.

Beyond local assistance and acknowledgement from the likes of the clergy and prominent citizens, there was little other support, certainly not from the government. 'Spreading alarm and despondency' was a crime and the subject of sexual disease a grey area in every-day discourse. Only one thing mattered – the war must be won.

The fateful day is coming

By the end of 1943, the Allies knew that 'Overlord' – codename for the liberation of France – was coming: exactly when was more difficult to say. Churchill called for a Second Army of six divisions.

The coastal area of Norfolk and ports to the south became a training area. Vast swathes of land were requisitioned – in 1942 9,000 acres behind Orford Ness in Suffolk had already been taken over with the loss of homes for 450 residents. Now farms were taken over where needed as well as an extensive area north of Southwold, also in Suffolk. In this area mines previously laid to prevent invasion were partially taken out and then, to save time and laborious work, it was decided to run Churchill tanks up and down over the land to explode the remainder.

By late 1943, Norfolk was full of troops practising assaults on areas previously erected with scaffolding, ditches, wire fencing and pillboxes to deter invasion and now suddenly perfect for the training of British troops. The areas behind Gorleston and North Denes beach at Yarmouth were used and there were secret exercises around Thetford and King's Lynn.

Minesweepers were busy clearing a path for the invading troops and Horsa gliders for the airborne troops were produced in such numbers by workers on East Anglian bomber airfields – many hundreds were quickly built – that storing them invisibly was a major exercise. The RAF as a whole was also being transformed from a defending force to an attacking one. The Americans, too, were recruiting and training new air crew. In September came the Great Deception, part of which was a mock invasion of France codenamed 'Starkey'.

Norfolk troops also trained for the future invasion – the 7th Battalion of the Royal Norfolks had actually spent the summer of 1943 in Kent but began to shift training priorities along with most battalions of the East Anglian regiments. In the forthcoming assault, the 1st Royal Norfolks and the 1st Suffolks were assigned to go ashore first, alongside Americans and Canadians. Training for beach landings was transferred to the lochs of Scotland in the summer. Another battalion of the Royal Norfolks, the 9th, were at this time assisting in the running of camps along the south coast.

The seventeen battalions of the Home Guard in Norfolk were in fine heart. They were far removed from the image of 'Dad's Army' by this time, the average age being just above thirty, and they were well-equipped and kitted out. But what could they do in the forthcoming operations? What could be their role? Now that the biggest assault of the war was being planned, there was no need to guard all those bridges and mount roadblocks at home. Some began to feel that they were surplus to requirements and feared for their continued existence.

Starting to plan for a post-war Norfolk

Great Yarmouth and the coastal towns reflected the national mood that victory was coming and began to prepare plans for rebuilding, with claims for compensation figuring highly, once hostilities ceased. Norwich, badly battered, appointed a consultant, Mr F. Longstreth Thompson, to work with others on building 'a beautiful and convenient city'. Norfolk's farmers, too, were concerned with many things, one being that the super-human efforts demanded from them had affected the fertility of the soil. All these concerns and plans would have to wait a little longer than anticipated to be addressed and put into action, however, as final victory was not to come, despite General Eisenhower's famous claim, in 1944.

Some Norfolk Soldiers, Sailors, Airmen and Civilian Dead

Patrick Arnott, Sergeant (Air Bomber) 1333984, 15 Squadron, Royal Air Force Volunteer Reserve, was killed on 25 May 1943, aged 19. He was the son of Frederick Henry and Nellie Arnott

HMS Welshman.

of Holt, Norfolk. He is buried in Jonkerbos War Cemetery, Netherlands.

Ronald Douglas Bond, Leading Aircraftman 541180, Royal Air Force, was killed on 1 February 1943, aged 23. He was serving on HMS *Welshman* when it was torpedoed by *U-617* with the loss of 150 Naval crew and a number of Air Force and Army personnel. Ronald Bond was the son of Bertie and Eunice Bond of Holt, Norfolk. He has no known grave and is commemorated on Malta Memorial.

Peter William Framingham, Private 5772825, 5th Battalion, Royal Norfolk Regiment, died 29 June 1943, aged 21. He was the son of Mr and Mrs F.P. Framingham of Hunstanton, Norfolk. He is buried in Kanchanaburi War Cemetery, Thailand.

Sidney Martin Hattersley M.C., Croix de Guerre, Colonel, Royal Army Medical Corps, died 24 March 1943, aged 55. He was the son of Isaac and Rosine Hattersley and husband of Vera Hattersley of Overy Staithe, Norfolk. He is buried in the churchyard of St Clement, Burnham Overy Staithe.

HMS Eskimo.

Anthony Duncan Herbert Hawley, Flying Officer. Pilot Royal Air Force Volunteer Reserve was the son of George and Eileen Hawley of Brancaster. He died on Friday, 9 July 1943 aged 20 and is buried in La Reunion War Cemetery, Algeria.

William George Love, Civilian War Dead, Air Raid Warden, aged 38, died 7 May 1943 at Great Yarmouth. He lived at 45 High Mill Road, Southtown.

Gordon Mayes, Private 5779227, 6th Battalion, Royal Norfolk Regiment, died as a prisoner of war of the Japanese while working on the Burma Railway 19 September 1943, aged 23. He was the son of Sidney and Ellen Mayes of Tacolneston, Norfolk and is buried in Chungkai Cemetery, Thailand.

William Raymond Myhill, Sergeant Wireless Operator/Air Gunner, 75th Squadron, Royal Air Force Volunteer Reserve, died on Sunday, 24 October 1943. Following a successful mine-laying mission, his Stirling Mk III bomber overshot the runway at Mepal in Cambridgeshire and four of the seven crew were killed. He had attended Acle School and worked at the Co-op. He is buried in the churchyard at Acle.

Albert Edward Charles Nason, Petty Officer, Sick Berth Attendant C/M 36075 HMS *Eskimo*, Royal Navy, was killed 12 July 1943, aged 40. His ship was in the Mediterranean when struck by a bomb which detonated the fuel tanks, killing or injuring nineteen. Albert Nason was the son of Alfred and Jessie Nason and husband of Ellen Nason, all of Swaffham, Norfolk.

Sidney Edward Woodhouse, Corporal 1230094, 521 Squadron, Royal Air Force Volunteer Reserve, died on 3 September 1943, aged 39. He was the son of Herbert and Deborah Woodhouse and husband of Marion Marie Woodhouse, of Holt, Norfolk. He is buried in Holt Burial Ground.

Jack Rowland Wales, Sergeant 1496737, 100 Squadron, Royal Air Force Volunteer Reserve, died on 4 September 1943, aged 22. Lancaster III JA930 HW-Y set off from Grimsby just before 8.00 pm tasked with bombing Berlin where the aircraft exploded. Jack Wales was the son of Walter and Elsie Wales of Worstead, Norfolk and he is commemorated on Runnymede Memorial, Surrey.

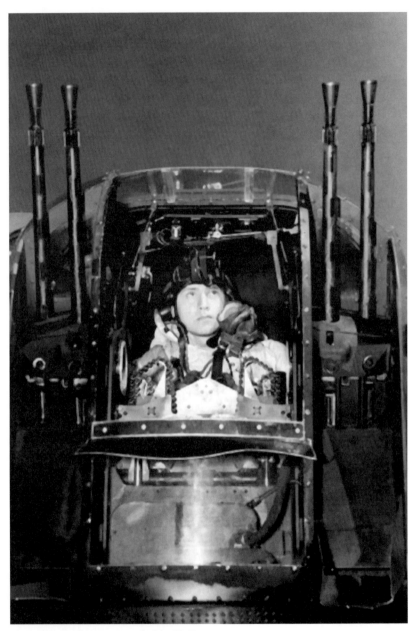

Lancaster tail gunner, probably 1943.

CHAPTER SIX

1944

At A Glance: Local and World events

JANUARY

Local
Preparations for D-Day. New evacuees.

World
Russians cross Polish border. Eisenhower appointed C-in-C Allied Expeditionary Force. Allies begin advance in Salerno.

FEBRUARY

Local
Raids from Norfolk bases for 'Big Week'.

World
Germans seek to take Anzio beachhead.

MARCH

Local
Water shortage due to dry weather.

World
Further Russian successes.

APRIL

Local

New coastal access restrictions. Airfield construction completed in Norfolk.

MAY

Local

East Anglian regiments prepare for invasion.

World

Allies capture Cassino and Russians occupy Sebastopol.

JUNE

Local

First V1s reach land. Soham ammunition train explodes. People are encouraged to take 'Farm holidays'.

World

D-Day. Americans capture Saipan island. Allies occupy Rome. Imphal road cleared of Japanese. Heavy losses imposed on Japanese Navy.

JULY

Local

New wave of evacuees from London arrive in Norfolk.

World

Caen taken. Russians capture Brest-Litovsk.

AUGUST

Local

Beer runs out in some places. Ban on coastal access partially lifted.

World

Paris liberated. American HQ moved to France. Japanese driven from India. Germans on retreat from Florence. Warsaw uprising.

SEPTEMBER

Local

First V2 rockets reach East Anglia. Invasion committees stood down.

World

Unsuccessful Allied airborne landings at Arnhem. France liberation complete. US troops enter Germany. Belgium and Luxembourg liberated.

OCTOBER

Local

Successful counter of V2s in East Anglia.

World

Allies enter Greece and occupy part of Holland. De Gaulle establishes French government.

NOVEMBER

Local

Coastal resorts begin to enter 'post-war-mode'. Sign posts put back in Norfolk. Ice-cream once again available.

World

Allied successes include capture of Metz. US bombs Tokyo. Roosevelt re-elected.

DECEMBER

Local

Home Guard disbanded. More news received of prisoners-of-war in Japanese hands.

World

Red Army surrounds Budapest. Germans attempt unsuccessful counter-attack in Belgium. British fight in Greece.

Everyday life, rations and local crime

In Norfolk, troops swarmed everywhere. They were billeted in private homes and commandeered buildings, they packed the pubs and restaurants, their armoured vehicles manoeuvred through the villages, they were the exclusive residents of large stretches of the coastline and, in the skies above, the planes of the RAF and the USAAF hardly ever ceased their missions both day and night.

For the Norfolk citizen, rations were still tight, although some restrictions were lifted. The cheese ration, for example, was cut from 3oz per head per week to 2oz but the weekly milk ration was increased from 2 to 2½ pints. You could have a double-breasted suit now, even with turn-ups and (almost) white bread was available for a price. Beer was not always in the pubs for the workers after a hard day in the fields but there were sometimes 'bonus' increases of certain foods, for example, the bacon ration was increased to 6oz from 4oz for a few weeks during harvest time.

The government continued to try to take money out of circulation with fund raising campaigns, the major one for 1944 being 'Salute the Soldier' week – Norwich raised £1,603,725 and Great Yarmouth £365,000. The war was apparently costing £13,250,000 a day by now, according to the government.

Serious crime was rare. There were numerous cases of 'fraternization' by young women and Italian prisoners of war which was technically illegal. Common-sense generally prevailed and there was a call for women police officers to deal with troubled or drunk girls and women. Also, the fact that there were a great many black Americans and that the authorities on both sides feared making hard-and-fast rules about fraternization of different races led to confusion. On the whole, however, the people of Norfolk were very relaxed about having guests of any nationality in their midst. This was remarkable in that just a few years before, much of rural Norfolk was almost a separate country from even the rest of England.

One sensational criminal case occurred late in the year when two American GIs, following a heavy drinking session on 3 December, decided to break into an armoury and go poaching in a wood near Honingham Hall, Norwich. Sir Eric Teichman heard shots in his wood and, on investigating, was shot dead. A 27-year-old from Pittsburgh was court-martialled – all alleged crimes involving American forces were dealt with by the military – and sentenced to death.

Cyril Joe Barton VC.

Pilot Officer Cyril Joe Barton VC, Benjamin Gimbert GC and William Nightall GC

On 30 March Pilot Officer Cyril Joe Barton, a Suffolk man, was in flight 70 miles short of his target, which was Nuremberg, when he was attacked by German fighters. He lost all communication with his team but carried on and released the bombs accurately. On running short of fuel when he returned to England, his navigator, bomb aimer and radio-operator baled out and he crash-landed the aircraft on one engine. The six other members of the crew survived but he was killed. For this action, he was awarded the Victoria Cross.

Sometimes bombs exploded accidentally before being loaded. On one occasion, one of the trucks of a supply train at Soham in Cambridgeshire caught fire and exploded, total disaster being averted only due to the bravery of the driver, Benjamin Gimbert, who was injured and the fireman, 21-year-

Memorial in the Anglican Cathedral, Norwich.

Roll of Honour in Saint Giles Church, Norwich.

1914 - 1918
WILLIAM OSWALD WEIR
NORMAN WELTON
DAVID E H WOODS
ERNEST H YARE
GEOFFREY W YOUNGMAN
PERCY YOUNGS

1939 - 1945
FREDERICK ANDREWS
WILLIAM BROWNE
CHARLES BREEZE
ERNEST BUCKLE
ERNEST COGMAN
FRANK COOPER
ALGERNON CUBITT
FRANK ETTELIDGE
HAROLD FISHER
WALTER FISHER
MAURICE GAYMER

1939 - 1945
PERCY HARDY
GORDON HENSLEY
CHARLES HILTON
CHARLES KETTERINGHAM
FREDERICK LAKE
PERCY LINCOLN
WALTER OSBORNE
DOUGLAS PALMER
EDWARD PETLEY
PETER RAMM
WILLIAM SHIELDS
ARTHUR WARNER
RAYMOND WOODCRAFT
1950 - 1953
KOREAN WAR
RAYMOND MAURICE PERFECT

TO THE
GLORY OF GOD
AND IN HONOURED
MEMORY OF THE MEN
OF ATTLEBOROUGH
WHO DIED IN THE
SERVICE OF THEIR
COUNTRY

The War Memorial in Attleborough with close-up (top).

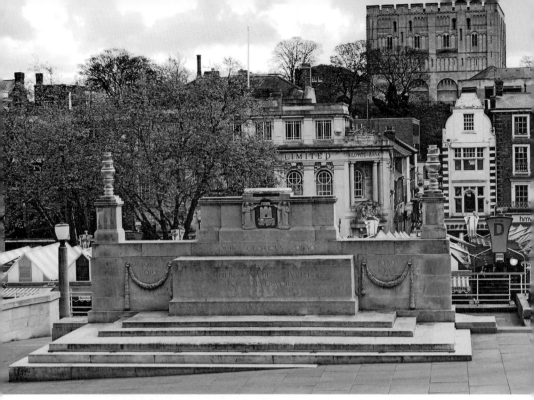

War memorial, Norwich City Centre. The Market is in the 'dip' and the Castle to the top right. The memorial was designed by Sir Edwin Lutyens, who also designed the Cenotaph in London. It was rededicated in 2010, following a £2.6 million restoration, using exactly the same words as were used on its inauguration in 1927. It was turned around to face the street at this time.

Memorial at Trinity Church, Loddon.

Memorial to all Gurkha soldiers in Great Yarmouth.

Tower of St Clement, Colegate, Norwich.

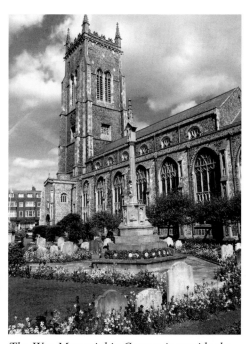

The War Memorial in Cromer is outside the Church of St Peter and St Paul. There are further memorials made of brass and wood inside the church.

Memorial, St Michael's Church, Aylsham.

Holt: the memorial is in the main street.

Great Yarmouth Memorial for both world wars.

Glass window to the Norfolk Regiment in St Nicholas Church, Great Yarmouth.

old William Nightall, who was killed. Both were awarded the George Cross.

Memorials

Norfolk, as elsewhere, has memorials to the dead of both world wars in every town and village. They are of stone, wood, glass, silk, paper and steel, ranging from projects designed by famous architects costing thousands of pounds to simple painted scrolls. Often, the memorial to those who died in the Great War has been extended in some way.

Many of the memorials are now protected – that at St Edmunds, Costessey, Norwich is one such, given Grade II listed status in 2017.

Loss of aircraft, accidents and bombing raids; The Big Week

Many planes were lost in accidents at home. In January, a Flying Fortress caught fire on take-off from Ridgewell in Essex. The pilot dumped its bombs and tried to find a field in which to land but, sadly, clipped some trees, killing all ten crew. Other pilots tried to miss houses when the engines went dead or, in one case, on hitting a power line and flipping. On 29 March two Liberators collided in mid-air over Henham Park, Suffolk.

Losses on raids were terrible. In the raid on Leipzig on 19/20 February the RAF lost 44 Lancasters and 34 Halifaxes. On 31 March it lost 94 out of the 795 bombers sent to attack Nuremberg. In five months Bomber Command lost 1,047 planes – a complete disaster. No hint of these losses reached the public, the local press being careful to talk only of Allied successes. However, a comprehensive re-evaluation of strategy of bomber streams was undertaken – raids by 800 planes should henceforth be able to arrive and drop bombs over targets within twenty minutes. A new bomber support group took over some airfields in North Norfolk. By the spring the RAF had largely

CLACTON
NAZI RAIDER CRASH!

Every Family is urged to take immediate
advantage of

"JOHN BULL'S"
£200 AIR RAID
INSURANCE
(Underwritten at LLOYDS)

FREE!
FOR EVERY READER

JOHN BULL
EVERY THURSDAY - 2d.

★ *Fill in the Newsagent's Order Form on right now and hand it to your newsagent as soon as possible. Fill in the Registration Form also and post it at once to "John Bull."*

SIGN TO-DAY

JOHN BULL
Hand this Form to Your Newsagent.

To (Name of Newsagent) ....

Address ....

Please deliver or reserve JOHN BULL for me weekly until further notice.

Signature ....

Address ....

....

Date ....

PLEASE WRITE CLEARLY.
C.G. 3 5 1940

POST THIS FORM TO
John Bull," Registration Department, 138, Long Acre, London W C 2

I have sent an Order Form to my Newsagent for the regular weekly delivery of JOHN BULL. Please register me as a regular reader.

Reader's Signature
Age...............

Address ....

....

Name and Address of Newsagent

....

Use 1d. stamp. Don't seal envelope. A Certificate setting out the full Benefits and Conditions and certifying registration will be sent if 1d. stamped addressed envelope is enclosed for return.

PLEASE WRITE CLEARLY. C.G. 3 5 1940

Free insurance offered to Clacton residents!

Lancaster Bomb Bay.

Avro Lancaster over Hamburg.

Bouncing-bomb, with chain to give it
backspin, on a Lancaster, 1944.

Lancaster dropping incendiaries and a 'cookie' bomb, 1944.

overcome its difficulties and gained daylight supremacy over Germany.

> *'If you're going through hell, keep going.'*
>
> Winston Churchill

America's 'Mighty Eighth' began to probe further into Germany. It dropped 6,000 tons of bombs in 3,300 sorties in one seven-day period in February – the targets were submarine bases, supply trains, bridges, aircraft factories and oil dumps. This was known as 'The Big Week'. They then turned their attention to Berlin, launching attacks in March which deployed 700 bombers. Losses were high at around 10 per cent.

Group Captain Percy Pickard DSO

Lancasters bomb St Vith in the Ardennes, 1944.

The crew, technical support, fuel and armaments for a Lancaster.

A legendary flyer, commanding officer at Sculthorpe in Norfolk, was Group Captain Percy Charles Pickard. He was an old boy of Framlingham College, Woodbridge, Suffolk and was the first officer to win the DSO three times in one war. He developed an excellent communication system with the French Resistance and was the obvious choice to lead a force of eighteen Mosquito fighter-bombers on an attack on the walls of Amiens prison. The object was to breach the walls and thus enable prisoners to escape – this included a prominent Resistance fighter awaiting imminent execution. The plan partially succeeded as the walls were breached but a great many prisoners were killed trying to escape. Group Captain Pickard was shot down and killed.

All through the first half of 1944 American personnel and machines flowed cross the Atlantic and in less than a year the Eighth Air Force doubled its size. Three bomb groups arrived, including one at Horsham St Faiths (now Norwich International Airport). Eventually a point was reached in 1944 when all needs

Wing Commander Percy Pickard in 1942.

of the US air chiefs had been met and no more airfields were constructed in Norfolk or the eastern counties.

German air raids continued but on a much lesser scale than in 1943: in the first three months of 1944 there were twenty night raids and fifteen people were killed. Most German attacks headed for London now.

The Royal Norfolks in Burma

At the beginning of the year, the Japanese were launching attacks in Arakan, Burma and the 2nd Battalion of the Suffolk Regiment was heavily engaged in what, for the Japanese, turned out quickly to be a fruitless exercise, abandoned at the

John Neil Randle VC.

end of February. During this period some members of the Royal Norfolk Regiment distinguished themselves also, one being Lieutenant D. Lee Hunter, a young officer whose bravery and dash in organizing the hacking through of almost impenetrable jungle was greatly admired.

The Japanese continued to threaten the vital supply town of Imphal, inside the Indian border and, in March, the 2nd Battalion of the Royal Norfolk Regiment and the 1st Battalion of the Essex Regiment, were flown in to back up the Suffolks. The Royal Norfolks were immediately dispatched to relieve the garrison at Kohima. They then joined the operation beginning in April to drive the Japanese out of the country – this was not achieved until 25 August.

Captain John N. Randle VC

During heavy jungle fighting, troops in a Japanese bunker spraying deadly machine gun fire held up the Royal Norfolks. Twenty-six-year-old Captain John N. Randle charged the bunker single-handed and, though mortally wounded, managed to get close enough to throw a grenade into the bunker through a gun-slit. He then sealed off the gun-slit with his own body. The whole road became passable now and the area was captured. Captain Randle became one of four Royal Norfolk recipients of the Victoria Cross: his medal is currently on loan to the Imperial War Museum. The Royal Norfolks were at this point suffering from dysentery and fatigue and had lost 790 men and 7 officers in their fighting around Kohima: those that remained, just 14 officers and 366 other ranks, were now rested. By May, with the Japanese in retreat, the Royal Norfolks had recovered

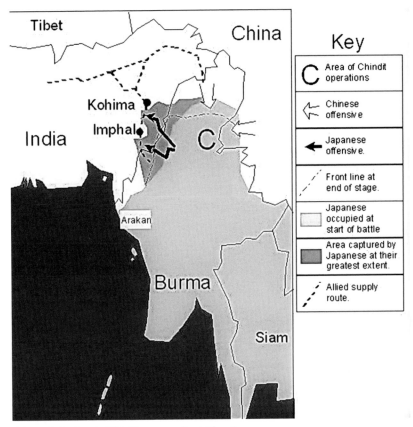

Map of the Imphal/Kohima area by Mike Young.

sufficiently to chase the defeated enemy down the Kohima–Imphal road. The Japanese invasion of India had collapsed with the loss of probably 65,000 men.

Operation 'Overlord': when and how?

Britain, Russia and America agreed at the conference in Tehran in November 1943 that a full-scale assault upon the coast of France – code-named 'Overlord' – should take place and, at Russia's insistence, it was agreed that the end of May 1944 should mark the launch. General Dwight Eisenhower was appointed Supreme Commander of the invasion forces and

British soldiers use 3-inch mortar fire in the Battle of Imphal-Kohima in March 1944.

General Bernard Montgomery was to be in charge of all Allied ground troops.

> *'I hate war as only a soldier who has lived it can, one who has seen its brutality, its stupidity.'*
>
> General Eisenhower

Montgomery visited the training camps in Scotland where the 1st Suffolks and 1st Royal Norfolks were scaling the loch sides as a substitute for the beaches of France. Sometimes they went out to sea in rough weather to practise landings. The Norfolks were also training for room-to-room fighting, in anticipation of their invasion role, using the houses of Aberdeen. Of the war, Montgomery confided to the troops, 'I am getting fed up with the thing. I think it is nearly time we finished it.'

Churchill fires a Thompson submachine gun beside General Eisenhower before Operation Overlord.

Eisenhower, meanwhile, toured the US bases in Norfolk and the eastern counties. In March, Churchill announced 'The hour of our greatest effort and action is approaching.' In April and May a series of meetings between Churchill and Eisenhower was held at St Paul's School, London after which the Supreme Commander of the invasion forces made his oft-quoted remark that Hitler had 'missed his one and only chance of destroying with a single well-aimed bomb the entire high command of the Allied forces.'

It was decided at these meetings that the 1st Royal Norfolks, and the 7th in following up, should be amongst the first troops to land in France. By the end of May an invasion fleet of nearly 7,000 craft was assembled. The RAF and USAAF were at the

Douglas bomber of 416 Group in flames over France, 12 May 1944.

same time launching a total of 144,800 bomber missions, losing 1,616 bombers and 12,000 men. In contrast, the Germans made about 120 reconnaissance missions over Britain in this period.

At home on the Norfolk coast, a 'protected area' was declared from the Wash to Land's End – if you did not live there you could not enter under any circumstances and, if you did, you went about your business and made no comment to anyone about what was going on. Identity cards were needed at all times. This applied to all the coastal towns including King's Lynn, Cromer, Sheringham, the Runtons, Great Yarmouth and Lowestoft.

At the end of May troops began to move – the Royal Norfolks to Haywards Heath, the 1st Suffolks to Horndean, Portsmouth and the 2nd Essex to Beaulieu. Men were encouraged to write their Wills.

Finally, after months of waiting, Eisenhower announced that D-Day was to be on 5 June. The weather, however, forced a postponement. The Allied invasion of Europe went ahead

24-hours later, beginning at 3.00 am with an armada of 1,000 RAF bombers from bases in Norfolk and the south of England.

Tuesday, 6 June 1944: D-Day; Landings of the Royal Norfolks, the Suffolks and the Essex Regiment

That the long-awaited assault had begun was announced in Britain on the midday news. It had actually started nine hours earlier with the RAF bombing German coastal defences in France. Virtually every airfield in Norfolk took part – a Group would fly out, bomb their assigned target, return to base, refuel, re-equip and go out once again. The skies were black with aircraft, the noise of the engines non-stop. What was happening was obvious to everyone.

Following this, at just after 5.00 am, 140 warships took over the bombardment, each ship concentrating on a previously agreed shore battery.

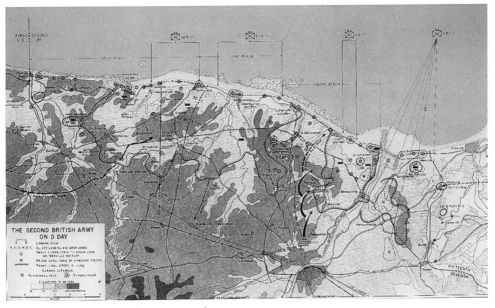

American map of D-Day Landings.

The British and Americans flew 14,000 sorties on the day – this against just 250 by Germany. Some were intended to mislead the enemy into thinking the attack was centred on the Pas de Calais.

The landings by 3rd Division, including the Royal Norfolks and Suffolks were on a sparsely populated – around 2,800 people lived there – 7-mile stretch of coast near Ouistreham: named 'Sword' beaches. The 2nd Battalion of the Essex Regiment was assigned to 'Gold' beaches from which they intended to make a dash to Bayeux. The 3rd Canadian Division was given 'Juno' beaches.

As regards rations, each man had supplies for 48 hours in two separate 24-hour waterproof packages. They had biscuits, oatmeal blocks, tea, sugar and milk blocks, dehydrated meat, chocolate, sweets, chewing gum, meat extract cubes and salt. They had a 'Tommy' cooker, a waterproof tin with matches, twenty 'Players' cigarettes and four vomit bags. After that, it was up to the cooks on the ground.

Montgomery wanted Caen taken as soon as possible and each Division had their own tasks on the way to this objective.

The Royal Norfolks embarked at Newhaven, the 1st Suffolks at Portsmouth and the 2nd Essex at Lymington. The invasion fleet anchored about 7 miles out, the troops transferring to the eighteen assault craft carried by each infantry ship. This was about 6.00 am, and the Royal Norfolks landed about 1½ hours later. They had a 'dry' landing as the craft could get close in to the beach. There were no casualties.

For the Suffolks the story was completely different as they had to wade waist-deep for 30 yards in the face of a German assault by mortars and shells. Once on the beach they had to deal with snipers. They had assembled at their appointed place near Hermanville-sur-Mer, about 1½ miles inland, by 9.30 am. They then pushed forward to attack a German headquarters, codenamed 'Hilman'. This was a huge task with resistance crumbling only at about 8.15 pm after which they dug in for the night. They had lost two officers and five other ranks with twenty-five injured.

The Norfolks had to push past them and reached their objective – called 'Norfolk House' – at about 7.00 pm. The weather was warm and sunny and they were cheered to see gliders coming over the skies with reinforcements. They had suffered one officer and thirteen other ranks killed.

The 2nd Battalion of the Essex Regiment reached within a mile and a half of their objective, Bayeux, and were digging in by 9.30 pm. Their only losses were four wounded by sniper fire.

The landings were deemed a success. The Germans were undoubtedly fooled into thinking that the main attack was to be in the Pas de Calais. Rommel was away visiting his wife on her birthday, convinced that the weather was unsuitable for an invasion. By the time the German Supreme Command realized that the landings were indeed happening, it was too late to respond more effectively.

Take Caen!

By this time, 130,000 ground troops and 23,000 airborne troops had been landed. By the end of June, this total had risen to a million men. Montgomery wanted a quick capture of Caen. Bayeux, just 4 miles away, was taken by the 2nd Battalion of the Essex Regiment immediately but Caen was not to fall until 9 July.

The Royal Norfolks were meanwhile fighting around 'Norfolk House': a battalion was to remain there for all of June.

On 11 June a plan was made to encircle Caen but this was abandoned following a blitz by a German SS Panzer Corps. A new attempt to outflank Caen on the west from 26–30 June resulted in dismal failure with 4,020 casualties. Another attack on villages north of Caen by troops including the 1st Suffolks was almost simultaneously beaten off. An all-out siege became unavoidable and this, which involved the 7th Norfolks in heavy fighting, finally succeeded on 9 July. The guns of HMS *Warspite* offshore preceded the storming of the walls. Caen, a previously beautiful city of 60,000, was 70 per cent destroyed with both the cathedral and university obliterated. It took fourteen years to rebuild the university after the war.

Two people watch as a Canadian tank clears debris from the streets of Caen.

General Patton talking to wounded troops.

Across the River Orne

Elsewhere, meanwhile, the Americans were making good progress, capturing Cherbourg on 26 June. The Allied commanders now set their sights on crossing the River Orne, after which the countryside would be suitable for rapid tank

Sidney (Basher) Bates VC.

advances. An attack, involving the 1st Royal Norfolks and 1st Suffolks, was codenamed 'Goodwood' and began on 18 July with one of the most ferocious air and naval onslaughts ever attempted by the combined Royal Navy, RAF and USAAF. The operation failed and was cancelled on the day it began with the loss of 400 tanks and with over 5,000 casualties. The Norfolks were relieved on 25 July and relaxed as much as possible, playing some cricket and drinking the small amounts of beer available. A crucial success was that two vital crossings had now been independently made, one over the Odon and the other over the Orne. In many areas it was evident that German resistance was lessening.

General George S. Patton arrives

'May God Have mercy on my enemies, because I won't....'

General Patton

A massive southward thrust began from 25 July, involving the 7th Norfolks. Saturation bombing from East Anglian bases succeeded in weakening the enemy and, on 30 July, the Americans marched into Avranches. General George S. Patton's Third US Army now joined the US First Army and he was very soon racing, seemingly unstoppable, towards Paris. The Germans launched a desperate counter-attack which was defeated with great heroism being shown by the 7th Norfolks.

'Take that, you bastards, and that, and that.'
Sidney (Basher) Bates VC

It was at this time that a 24-year-old corporal in the Royal Norfolks won the Victoria Cross. Sidney 'Basher' Bates was advancing against the enemy when his machine gunner and best friend was killed. Seizing the light machine gun he ran towards the Germans, shooting from the hip, shouting: 'Take that, you bastards, and that, and that.' He was shot but his actions had a demoralizing effect upon the enemy as he fell, regained his feet and carried on advancing. He was shot again, fell and once more got to his feet at which the nonplussed enemy began to withdraw. He was hit by mortar splinters and fell to the ground for a final time, but continued to fire until he passed out. He died two days afterwards.

Captain David Jamieson, VC

Captain Jamieson, serving in the 7th Norfolks, was 23 years old, 6ft 5in tall and came from Thornham, King's Lynn. He was in command of a company which was fighting to maintain the Grimbosq bridgehead when the enemy destroyed two of the three tanks giving it support. Captain Jamieson rushed over to the remaining one and, having lost communications, clambered manually aboard in full view of the enemy. Following this, wounded in the right eye and arm, with all other officers having been lost, he walked among his men and reorganized the company, refusing to be evacuated. He stayed with his men during three further attacks that day. The 7th Norfolks eventually received a warm welcome when they reached Falaise which had been taken by the Canadians on 16 August. Falaise was a town of 5,000, previously famed for being the birthplace of William the Conqueror.

Ten thousand German soldiers perished in the co-called 'Falaise Pocket' where they were trapped. Fifty thousand were taken prisoner. This was a fatal blow leaving France wide open and almost undefended almost the entire way to Germany.

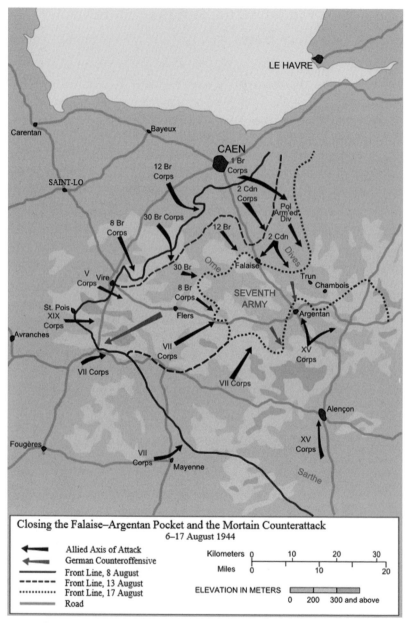

Closing the Falaise–Argentan Pocket and the Mortain Counterattack
6–17 August 1944

Map of troops at Falaise Pocket.

British troops give tea to German prisoners at Falaise.

The 7th Norfolks were officially disbanded to various regiments on 26 August, some of the men transferring to the 1st Suffolks and others to the 1st Royal Norfolks.

On the 70th anniversary of D-Day, the president of France announced that the Ordre National de la Légion d'Honneur would be awarded to all British veterans who fought for the liberation of France during the war.

Last throw of the German dice

Exactly one week after bombers took off from English airfields to begin the D-Day assault, a new weapon reached Britain – the 'flying bomb' or 'doodle-bug', twenty-seven in all, the first

Surrendering German troops at Falaise.

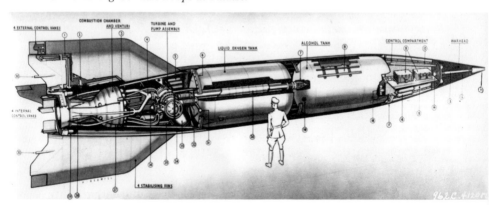

1 CHAIN DRIVE TO EXTERNAL CONTROL VALVE
2 ELECTRIC MOTOR
3 BURNER CUPS
4 ALCHOL SUPPLY FROM PUMP
5 AIR BOTTLES
6 REAR JOINT RING AND STRONG POINT FOR TRANSPORT
7 SERVO-OPERATED ALCOHOL OUTLET VALVE
8 ROCKET SHELL
9 RADIO EQUIPMENT
10 PIPE LEADING FROM ALCOHOL TANK TO WARHEAD

11 NOSE PROBABLY FITTED WITH NOSE SWITCH, OR OTHER DEVICE FOR OPERATING WARHEAD FUZE
12 CONDUIT CARRYING WIRES TO NOSE OF WARHEAD
13 CENTRAL EXPLODER TUBE
14 ELECTRIC FUZE FOR WARHEAD
15 PLYWOOD FRAME
16 NITROGEN BOTTLES
17 FRONT JOINT RING AND STRONG POINT FOR TRANSPORT
18 PITCH AND AZIMUTH GYROS
19 ALCOHOL FILLING POINT
20 DOUBLE WALLED ALCOHOL DELIVERY PIPE TO PUMP

21 OXYGEN FILLING POINT
22 CONCERTINA CONNECTIONS
23 HYDROGEN PEROXIDE TANK
24 TUBULAR FRAME HOLDING TURBINE AND PUMP ASSEMBLY
25 PERMANGANATE TANK (GAS GENERATOR UNIT BEHIND THIS TANK)
26 OXYGEN DISTRIBUTOR FROM PUMP
27 ALCOHOL PIPES FOR SUBSIDIARY COOLING
28 ALCOHOL INLET TO DOUBLE WALL
29 ELECTRO-HYDRAULIC SERVO MOTORS
30 AERIAL LEADS

Cut-out illustration of a V2.

A V1 on a Heinkel 111 H-22.

reaching Gravesend in the early morning of 13 June. Later, when they became more sophisticated, deadly and increasingly difficult to shoot down, they were known as V1s and V2s. The first one seen from the ground in Norwich flew harmlessly over the city on 26 June. On 6 July, Churchill reported that 2,750 had been launched but most either failed or were shot down: they had, however, during this time killed 3,600 civilians and destroyed 13,000 homes. From August, they were being launched from Holland and Belgium as the Allies overran France, as well as pick-a-back on low-flying Heinkels.

A massive and very successful programme was undertaken to bring guns and searchlights to the coast from Great Yarmouth to the Thames. Many of the gunners were girls from the ATS and two million pounds was spent to urgently build them decent accommodation in Nissen huts with shops and cinemas nearby. More than half of the V1s were shot down over the sea and others by fighters.

The V2s were much more deadly than their predecessors – they travelled faster than the speed of sound, the first one

Cut-away of V1.

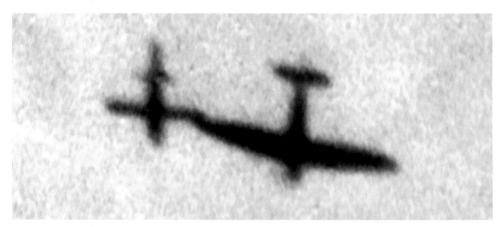

A Spitfire attempts to 'tilt' a V1 off-course.

landing at Chiswick in London on 8 September. The first in Norfolk hit Ranworth on 26 September; three more reached Horsford, Whitlingham and Beighton on 27 September; and three more exploded in Hemsby, Coltishall and Thorpe the next day. Most were aimed at London but some went seriously off-

Auxiliary Territorial Service Searchlight Unit.

course or were, as in the case of a major panic when one hit
Mundesley unexpectedly in October, way short of the mark.
Some just blew up mid-air. The people of Cromer had received
severe criticism during the Great War in that, according to the
Eastern Daily Press, citizens could not resist going outside to
witness the Zeppelins with their bombs passing overhead despite
the great peril; now, they were once again chastised as it was
possible to see, from Cromer seafront, the red streaks of V2s
launching in Holland and many needs must go and have a good
look. These missiles could not be shot down and so efforts were
made instead to launch bombing raids from Norfolk airfields
and elsewhere on their launch sites.

Lieutenant Joseph P. Kennedy Junior.

The Allies responded to the threats of the V1s and V2s by experimenting with their own 'drones' i.e. planes packed with explosives from which the pilots would parachute before the aircraft would carry on remotely to its specified target. One which went tragically wrong was piloted by Lieutenant Joseph P. Kennedy Junior – elder brother of the future President of the United States – and Lieutenant Wilford J. Willy. The two men were based at Winfarthing-Fersfield Army base in Norfolk and, on 12 August 1944, set out in a P4BY Liberator packed with 21,170 pounds of high explosive. The plane blew up at 15,000 feet over Blyth estuary causing damage over a 6-mile radius.

New evacuees; getting the food in

The new rockets prompted a renewed evacuation drive from London to East Anglia, the first party arriving on Friday, 14 July. Three thousand more arrived by train during July in Norwich, Diss, King's Lynn, Thetford and Lowestoft. Great Yarmouth, which had previously sent many people inland, was now expected to offer homes. Reception arrangements and attitudes were varied but often unenthusiastic. Many felt that they had been 'burned' before and had no wish to repeat the experience: the press carried letters from an aggrieved man who had offered his house fully furnished to a family who had subsequently left taking all the furniture with them; another claimed to have received a lady who had refused to lift a finger as 'the government was paying' for her keep, including all meals, washing etc.

Then all further group evacuation suddenly stopped – in the first week of September the government considered that the flying bomb menace was over. Although there was no need for a sudden departure, thousands rushed back to London, anxious to return to the life they knew.

Farming in East Anglia was in a very healthy state in 1944 – wheat, oats, peas, sugar-beet and potatoes were either at record production levels or about to be. Acreage had increased in Norfolk by very large amounts – as much as 70 per cent over pre-war levels in some cases. Cattle were about 25 per cent up in numbers, but some flocks of sheep and herds of pigs were given up due to the shortage of feed. Machines were, to the chagrin of many traditionalists, taking over the jobs of horses in some cases and electricity was beginning to spread to more and more remote villages.

Labour was a main problem. The government tried to encourage people to spend their holidays at a 'farm camp': pay was modest but a rail voucher and extra clothing coupons were on offer. The army was no longer allowed to help. The scheme was successful in some places, especially Suffolk.

Then there were the Italian prisoners – 50,000 of them in East Anglia as a whole. Upon the surrender of the Italian government in 1943 these prisoners were given the chance to enrol in an Italian labour corps. They had special uniforms, were organized like a military unit and had Italian NCOs. Not everyone was convinced about the reorganization, especially when one camp went on strike during the harvest period. They had many privileges previously denied – they could talk to civilians, accept invitations to people's houses, ride bicycles, enter shops, and go to cinemas. They could not, however, go to pubs or dance halls. There were also increasing numbers of German prisoners – 95,000 by October 1944. They were much more difficult to deal with – they were the sworn enemy, unlike the Italians who were now officially on Britain's side – and were consequently closely guarded. Some broke out of the camps and made a sprint for the coast and home but most did not as conditions for them were not at all bad: they had food and were even paid a (small-which-could-only-be-spent-in-the-camp-shop) wage for jobs.

Farmers were not happy, however, about several things – the fixed price for their produce being one of them and the lack of nutrients in the over-ploughed soil being another. The National Union of Agricultural Workers under its President, Edwin Gooch, was on the rise and celebrating record membership.

Military progress as the year ends: the 1st Suffolks and 1st Norfolks

Late summer saw some excellent news from the Allies' standpoint. Four Allied armies closed in to the Seine and Paris was liberated on 25 August. British and American bombers continued their raids from East Anglian bases. Some bomber groups of the US Ninth Air Force began to operate from France – the 332nd,

German officers sat in the Hotel Majestic, Paris having surrendered.

Liberation of Paris scene.

391st, 410th and the 416th. The Allies rapidly occupied the whole of France. The Allies made such gains on other fronts, and so quickly, that they outran their supply lines and it was not until Antwerp was wrested from a stubborn and tenacious German force by the end of November, that the supply route functioned properly again.

The 1st Suffolks and 1st Norfolks remained where they were based, not entirely contentedly as they now had a taste for glory after their pivotal contribution to D-Day successes in Normandy. There was relief when, in mid-September, they were called forward to become part of a new offensive, north-eastwards towards the River Maas and, hopefully, the German frontier. They travelled through France and Belgium as heroes,

Troops land in Holland.

101st Airborne inspect crashed glider.

Nijmegen after the battle 28 September, 1944.

British troops cross the bridge at Nijmegen.

Waffen SS prisoners at Nijmegen.

being given fruit, flowers, chocolate and cigarettes by the cheering locals.

Montgomery wanted to drive on and cross the Rhine at Arnhem and thus cut off the German army. On 16–18 September the biggest airborne force of the war invaded Holland. The Suffolks took the Dutch town of Weert and the Norfolks overran Helmond. Both enjoyed what comforts they could before they engaged in a bitter seven-day battle against a German bridgehead west of Maas: the Suffolks lost 1 officer, 18 other ranks killed and 144 wounded; the Norfolks suffered 211 casualties, among them 5 company commanders. Venraij was thereafter taken after stiff house-to-house fighting on 18 October. Both the

B-17G of the 8 AF 398 BG 601st BS, damaged on a raid over Cologne,
15 October 1944: the bombardier was killed.

B-17G of the 384th Bomb Group.

'Hell's Warrior': Liberator of 445 Bomb Group.

Suffolks and Norfolks were then able to gain some rest with a limited number of men released for leave.

The Essex battalion, meanwhile, crossed the River Mark and then was moved to Nijmegen which the Germans managed to flood before leaving, meaning that patrols were made in boats. Their year ended performing this duty.

The Americans took Metz and ended the year having broken the Ardennes offensive.

The air bases in Norfolk were now given the task of feeding the mainly starving citizens of Holland. They also kept up the offensives against Berlin, Hamburg, Leipzig and Munich – in one raid the 445th Bomb Group lost thirty aircraft in a day.

Bravery behind the lines

Men who were parachuted in behind the lines at this time often have no record or memorial as their missions were secret. One such was Major Andrew Croft, featured earlier. Sometimes they come to light afresh as is the case of Lieutenant Hugh Gurney, whose role has recently been featured in a book by a former SAS soldier. Lieutenant Gurney, from Northrepps, was twenty-six when he was sent from RAF Brize Norton to Rennes as part of a team of sixty SAS men. Sadly, he was shot a few weeks into the mission but is remembered as a lively, brave and capable soldier.

Beside A German Waterfall

Beside a German waterfall
On a very bright summer day
Beside a shattered airplane a navigator lay.
His pilot hung from a coconut tree
He was not yet quite dead
So listen to the very last words the navigator said.

We're going to a better land
Where everything's all right
Where whiskey flows from telephone poles
Play poker every night
We'll never have to work again
Just sit around and listen
We'll have beaucoup wild women
Oh death where is thy sting?

Anonymous

Searchlights over Norwich Cathedral, 1945.

Troops of the 1st Royal Norfolks in Wanssum, Holland, 26 November 1944.

Troops from Norfolk were engaged in other parts of the world also as the year ended. The 2nd Battalion of the Royal Norfolks were key in the bid by General Stilwell to sweep across the Chindwin River and advance into central Burma. This was a successful campaign proceeding by both river and land.

When Christmas came, families still sought news of the survivors from the Suffolk, Royal Norfolk and Cambridgeshire regiments that had surrendered at Singapore. The men that survived were now in many places occupied by the Japanese. Post cards home were wonderful for giving hope of life but useless in terms of news, always containing a variation of 'I am fine' and 'I am being treated well'. Such news as came back home

Men of the Suffolk Regiment surrender to the Japanese during the fall of Singapore.

was harrowing to the men's loved ones – usually this came from prisoners of war rescued and liberated from ships torpedoed by the Allies.

Amenities Ships

As 1944 progressed, the government became increasingly aware that, should the war continue, the troops farthest from home, especially those in the Pacific, would miss home comforts. A series of ten 'Amenities Ships' was originally planned where men could relax with good food, film shows and, importantly, drink beer. Beer from home did not travel well, so two former minelayers, HMS *Agamemnon* and HMS *Menestheus* were converted in Vancouver, each with an on-board brewery capable of producing 250 barrels of mild ale and bitter a week. Unsurprisingly, they often came to be called 'Brewery Ships'. Both the ships converted in Vancouver were ready for

HMS Agamemnon *as a minesweeper.*

service only as the war came to an end but, nevertheless, HMS *Menestheus* managed a short and much appreciated tour of naval bases in the region. The other eight planned Amenities Ships never saw the light of day.

Some relaxation at last, ice-cream, demobilization and leave for a few, the Home Guard stands down, and a Day of Prayer

People now believed that the war was soon to be won – the Germans were facing defeat on every front and the Japanese navy had lost control of the Pacific to the Americans.

In the summer, the ban on going to the seaside had already been lifted with trains and buses to Great Yarmouth, Hunstanton, Cromer and other resorts packed. From November some coastal towns were authorized to clear beach obstructions and the army began to take out mines. Many mines still exist today along the coast and the Coastguard is called out regularly, especially in recent years in the Scolt Head Island area.

There was a particular yearning for ice-cream, such that the Food Minister, Colonel Llewellin, allowed supplies to be made available for its manufacture. Road signs were put back – some pointing to the wrong places – and there was talk of what was reasonable in terms of public street lighting.

Some men were to be allowed to leave the forces – men of over fifty and those with sorely-needed skills such as housebuilding. Men would receive a suit, shirt, collars, tie, socks, shoes, a hat and a raincoat. Men over fifty would receive eight weeks' leave with full pay, plus additional leave for foreign service and be entitled to their old job back. Women in the auxiliary services would be treated in a similar way. General demobilization would not start, however, until the surrender of the Axis worldwide.

UK leave for the Liberation Army would begin on 1 January. Names would be drawn out of a hat where all things were equal. The invasion committees were stood down and, sadly for many, the Home Guard, who had long been fearing such an edict: each man was to return his tin hat, belts, ammunition, mess tin and water bottles. There were 1,141 officers and 30,541 Home Guard men in Norfolk and they were not going out without a bang – in Norwich 4,000 men turned up for the final ceremony while the Dorset Regiment Band played. They were further angered by controversy as to whether they were eligible to join the British Legion, many senior regular army officers believing that they certainly were not.

Other war organizations such as the National Fire Service were put on standby.

A National Day of Prayer was held on Sunday, 3 September in both Norwich cathedrals – the Cathedral of St John the Baptist

The Memorial to the dead of both wars on the external wall of St Peter Mancroft, Norwich.

Steps up and past St Peter Mancroft on a snowy winter day. The war memorial (of Christ on the Cross in the previous picture) is on the wall of the church in the section of graveyard immediately to the left just behind the metal railings. These railings are one of very few existing examples of the fancy ironwork of Boulton & Paul left in the city.

and the Cathedral Church of the Holy and Undivided Trinity. St Peter Mancroft rang out the peal in Norwich Market Place as it had done on every important occasion since the defeat of the Spanish Armada. There was a great deal of relief and happiness, even although Mr Churchill said that victory may not come until the summer of 1945. The only group who did not share some of this joy were the Norfolk families of the 1,500 prisoners held in German camps, the 2,000 in various camps in the Far East and the 600 posted missing.

The many thousands of German prisoners of war in Norfolk were deeply unpopular and were kept out of sight as much as possible.

Some Norfolk Soldiers, Sailors and Airmen

Charles Christopher Branch, Private 5827571, 2nd Battalion, Suffolk Regiment, died 29 September 1944 in India, aged 25. Imphal, in the War Cemetery of which Charles Branch lies, was a main fighting ground during the Japanese push towards India in the Spring of 1944. More details are given above in the main text. Private Branch was the son of Herbert and Violet Branch of Weeting, Norfolk.

John Edward Bush, Ordinary Signalman P/JX 389014, HMS *Janus*, Royal Navy, died 23 January 1944, aged 24. He was the son of May Louise Bush of Snettisham, Norfolk and has no known grave. He is commemorated on Portsmouth Naval Memorial, Hampshire. Note: HMS *Janus* was sunk by an aerial torpedo while involved in Operation 'Shingle' at Anzio.

HMS Janus.

James Frank Copeman, Drummer 2658383, Coldstream Guards, was killed on 18 June 1944, aged 22.The band was playing in the Guards' Chapel, Wellington Barracks when a German rocket shattered the roof, killing the conductor, Major Windram, and five musicians. He was the son of Archibald and Bertha Copeman of Tacolneston, Norfolk and husband of Bertha Coleman of Regents Park, London. He is buried in All Saints Churchyard, Tacolneston, Norfolk.

Raymond Alfred Harvey, Private, 4th Battalion, Royal Norfolk Regiment, died 15 September 1944 while at sea aboard the Japanese prison ship, *Rakuyo Maru*, which was torpedoed by the American submarine, USS *Sealion*. He was born in Norwich and enlisted there. He is commemorated on the Memorial in Kranji War Cemetery, Singapore.

Henry Graham Head, Major 100918, East African Artillery, Royal Artillery, 301 Field Regiment, died 12 February 1944, aged 25. He was the son of His Honour Judge Head and Geraldine Head of Overy Staithe, Norfolk. He had studied at Eton where he was Captain of School and gained a B.A. Hons (Oxon) from Balliol College. He is commemorated on the East Africa Memorial, Kenya.

Jack Playford, Pilot Officer, 175969, Royal Air Force Volunteer Reserve, DFM, was the son of Robert and Ethel Playford of Caister on Sea. He was killed in action aged 23 on 10 September 1944. He lies in Delhi War cemetery in India. His DFM citation reads: 'Warrant Officer Kelsey and Flight Sergeant Playford have participated in very many sorties. As observer and pilot respectively they have displayed great skill and their example of keenness and determination to engage the enemy has been worthy of high praise. They have destroyed 2 enemy aircraft'.

Albert Edward Hamilton Starman, Private, 5773302, 4th Battalion, Royal Norfolk Regiment, died at sea whilst on the *Tamahoku Maru* transport ship for prisoners of war. The ship was sunk by US torpedo bombers on 25 September 1944. Albert Starman was aged 25 and the son of Frank and Daisy Starman and husband of Wilma Starman of Thurlton, Norfolk. He is commemorated on the Singapore Memorial.

CHAPTER SEVEN

1945

At A Glance: Local and World events

JANUARY

Local

East Anglian Regiments holding front line on River Maas. Freezing weather to begin the year.

World

Red Army enters Warsaw. Armistice signed with Hungary.

FEBRUARY

Local

Norfolk soldiers enter Germany. Rehearsals for drop across Rhine.

World

Yalta Conference. Dresden raids. Red Army enters Budapest.

MARCH

Local

German air attacks on Norfolk end. Evacuees begin to return home.

World

US forces cross Rhine and capture Cologne. Britain takes Mandalay.

APRIL

Local

Norfolk and Suffolk soldiers in battle to capture Bremen. Heatwave. RAF and USAAF begin to bring back PoWs.

World

Surrender of all German armies in Italy. Mussolini killed. President Roosevelt dies. Concentration camps entered by Americans and British. Hitler shoots himself.

MAY

Local

V.E. Day. End of blackout. USAAF raise £20,000 for library at Norwich. Norwich issues '50 year plan'.

World

Unconditional surrender of all German forces. Channel Islands liberated. Rangoon recaptured. Norwegian government returns to Oslo. Dutch Royal family goes home.

JUNE

Local

Fishing resumes on East Coast. Many evacuees return to London.

World

United Nations Charter signed at San Francisco. Simla Conference

JULY

Local

Royal Navy closes base at Great Yarmouth. Huge fishing stocks taken.

World

Attlee forms new government. Potsdam Conference. US bombards Japan. Allied Control Commission takes over government of Berlin.

AUGUST

Local

V.J. celebrations. News arrives of Norfolk PoWs in Japanese camps. G.I. Brides Club formed in Norwich.

World

Atomic bombs dropped on Hiroshima and Nagasaki. Japan surrenders. British occupy Hong Kong.

SEPTEMBER

Local

Liberation of Norfolk PoWs in Far East. German prisoners work on harvest.

World

US Land-Lease ended. Mountbatten takes surrender of Japanese. New plan for India proposed.

OCTOBER

Local

PoWs come home to celebrations. Dutch children received into Norwich. East coast ports return to near normal operations.

World

UNO established.

NOVEMBER

Local

East coast resorts seek financial recompense from government.

World

Nuremberg trials. De Gaulle forms French government.

DECEMBER

Local

Norfolk farmers accused of running poultry black market. First Royal Christmas message since 1939.

World

Moscow Conference. US and Britain sign financial deal. Chiang Kai-shek re-enters Nanking.

The year begins: sweet and sour

As with the first year of the war, the last began in Norfolk with deep snow-drifts – around a foot of snow fell on Cromer – but now the situation was aggravated by electricity cuts and lack of coal supplies. Not even hospitals and factories escaped the shortages. However, spring came early and the daffodils bloomed as Norwich welcomed April with temperatures in the upper sixties. The symbolism was not lost to many or to the local press.

However, rationing continued and the V1s and V2s still came, the former launched from bombers over the North Sea. The Luftwaffe reappeared over Norfolk and Suffolk in March but ceased almost as soon as they began – the last bomb over Norfolk hit Swanton Morley at 9.30 pm on 20 March.

For the Allies, progress was swift into the German heartland but the celebrations were stifled by the horror of discoveries made – when the US 3rd Army occupied Buchenwald on 11 April they found 500 corpses piled in heaps and 20,000 living skeletons. The final act of the SS had been to wreck the water system. A few days later the British entered Belsen, near Hanover, and they discovered, actually or evidence of, over 35,000 corpses: it was reported that the SS had shot 2,000 the day before liberation. Some black and white footage of these terrors reached Norfolk cinema audiences.

At home, on 13 March, a 37-year-old leading aircraftsman was hanged at Norwich prison for the murder of a WAAF in Beccles.

June and July were hot but celebrations in Norfolk were muted, one reason being the thousands of men still unaccounted for who were in Japanese hands. This was despite V.E. Day in May and the fact that the war was undoubtedly coming to an end although the Japanese were not to surrender until August.

Norfolk bases and their final missions

After The Netherlands was liberated on 5 May, 50,000 children who were in a badly nourished state were brought over to Britain. Norwich accepted 500, aged ten to fifteen, in October and November. However, with the end of the war the Lend-Lease shipments of food from the United States ceased and there was talk of further bread rationing.

At the end of April, the bomber bases of East Anglia began a life-saving mission – feeding the starving Dutch and other people in dire need. They also began to fly prisoners home and to collect British soldiers. In one day alone – 8 May – 13,000 prisoners were flown from Europe to Britain.

At the same time, bombing missions continued, even increased. Air Chief Marshal Sir Arthur Harris was having disagreements with Sir Charles Portal, Chief of Air Staff, over tactics as the year began. Harris believed in 'area bombing' and devoted the main thrust of the attacks on German cities. The Americans joined in on twin missions – for example, joint bombing attacks were made on fourteen nights in January. Another big raid was on Wiesbaden which involved over 500 RAF bombers. Soon after, the US 8th Air Force sent the biggest fleet since D-Day to bomb Berlin. The Allies had almost total mastery of the skies by this time and encountered little opposition. Most of France was in Allied hands, but, when a German garrison held out at Royan the RAF sent Lancasters which destroyed four-fifths of the town, killed perhaps 800 French civilians but only about 35 Germans: there was further uproar about tactics.

One of the most controversial actions of the war took place on 13 and 14 February – the bombing of Dresden. The RAF made two separate raids, the first with 244 and the second with 529 Lancasters. The USAAF followed up with 311 B-17s and also Mustangs. The *East Anglian Daily Times* reported that 650,000 fire bombs had been dropped on the city and '…In the inner town not a single block of buildings, not a single detached building, remains intact…The town area is devoid of human life. A great city has been wiped from the map of Europe…' The MP for Ipswich, Richard R. Stokes, was horrified and even Churchill was reported to distance himself from the action, although in the end, supporting Harris.

Great damage was also done to other German historic towns, for instance, Worms, where 35,000 people lost their homes.

From mid-February Norfolk air bases began preparing for 'Operation Varsity', in which the RAF and USAAF were to assist the Rhine crossing. Horsa gliders over the county became common. In the event, once Montgomery had crossed the Rhine, the role of the planes was to drop food and medical supplies.

There was a great crescendo of activity at the end of March before the main role of the Norfolk airfields was done. For example, on 15 March, Berlin was raided by the entire US 8th Air Force and the RAF dropped 67,637 tons of bombs during the month – the greatest weight of any month in the war. Cologne, Essen, Wurzburg, Hanau, Hildesheim, and Dortmund were other targets. With the war clearly almost over in Europe, the bombers prepared to join the fight against Japan.

Men of the 4th, 5th and 6th battalions who had survived Japanese captivity at Aomi Hall, Japan 1945.

The Suffolks and the Royal Norfolks end their war

In January, the 1st Battalion of the Suffolks and the 1st Battalion of the Royal Norfolks were part of Montgomery's army holding the River Maas. On 6 January, the Royal Norfolks moved up to Meerlo and spent the remainder of the month patrolling in this area. By the beginning of March Allied armies were closing up to the Rhine and on 9 March the Americans entered Bonn. By this time the Americans had taken 343,000 German prisoners. Montgomery announced his plan for an assault crossing of the Rhine in the north with 80,000 men. This involved the 1st Battalion Royal Norfolks and the 1st Battalion Suffolks. On 23 March, Montgomery issued the order: '21 Army Group will now cross the Rhine.' Bombers and Para troops assisted and within a few days enemy resistance was broken. The advance to the Elbe resulted in the encirclement of the great industrial cities of the Rhur – Dusseldorf, Cologne, Essen, Munster, Dortmund, Duisburg, Wuppertal and Hamm. Some 325,000 German troops held out for eighteen days before surrendering. Thereafter, the Royal Norfolks entered Bremen, taking the best part of it within the hour. The war was over now as everyone knew and it was in Delmenhorst, whence they had relocated, that the Royal Norfolks heard news of the ceasefire. On 30 April Hitler shot himself in his bunker.

In the same week that Hitler committed suicide, the Japanese abandoned Rangoon. The 2nd Battalion of the Royal Norfolk Regiment had been training to help in the assault but in the event was not called upon as the taking of it was easier than expected.

Lieutenant George Arthur Knowland VC

The Royal Norfolks established a record in the British army with five Victoria Crosses being awarded during the conflict.

Men of the 3rd Division, Royal Norfolks, in house-to-house fighting in Kervenheim, Germany, 3 March 1945.

The last of these was to 22-year-old Lieutenant Knowland in heavy fighting near Kangaw on 31 January. With his twenty-four men under attack by 300 Japanese, he rushed from trench to trench continually firing any weapon he found – Bren gun mortar, tommy gun – and his men held on for twelve hours. He was killed but not before shooting or wounding a large number of the enemy and his actions were considered pivotal in preventing a counter-attack by the enemy.

The Norfolks moved to Mandalay which was finally captured on 9/10 March.

George Knowland VC.

The end and getting back home

On 8.15 am local time on 6 August, an atom bomb was dropped on Hiroshima. On 9 August another atom bomb was dropped on Nagasaki. The Japanese surrendered and the war was over. The main ceremony of surrender was on board the US battleship *Missouri* in Tokyo Bay on 2 September. Ten days afterwards, Lord Louis Mountbatten took the formal surrender of all Japanese forces within the South East Asia area command. The first man of the British occupation forces to walk upon Japanese territory was Lieutenant Colin Chapman, commander of the cruiser *Newfoundland*. He was from Norwich.

In Norfolk people now waited nervously for news of their menfolk who had been prisoners-of-war. After the Japanese surrender, there was little comfort until the local press announced on 1 September that 20,000 Singapore PoWs, including 6,500 Britons, were on their way home. All through September the

The mushroom cloud of the atomic bomb dropped on Nagasaki, 9 August 1945.

big news in the local papers concerned the prisoners who had been identified as coming home. Supplies were dropped on prison camps by the RAF. Some men came home via Rangoon and India, some by ship and a few by plane. On 7 October, the *Corfu* docked at Southampton and, amongst wild celebrations, off the decks came men from the Royal Norfolks, the Suffolks and the Cambridgeshires. They travelled to a transit camp where they were given medical examinations and then were put onto trains. The first Norfolk men arrived at Thorpe Station, Norwich, at about 10.00 pm – the train was twenty-nine minutes late, some previous shunting of empty carriages having mistakenly received enthusiastic applause – and were greeted by crowds all the way up Prince of Wales Road. The Lord Mayor, Mr S. A. Bailey, was there. More arrived the next day: many remarked on how fit and tanned they looked as they had obviously eaten very well on their homeward journey. It was only after they were back that the terrors of their captivity became apparent.

Some Norfolk Soldiers, Sailors and Airmen

Jack Dixon, Sergeant 1463894 W.Op./Air Gunner, 153 Squadron, Royal Air Force Volunteer Reserve, died on Tuesday, 6 March

1945. He was the son of Walter and Rosa Dixon who lived in East Ruston, Norfolk. He is buried in Prague War Cemetery.

John Kay England, Lieutenant, 255222, 8th Battalion, Royal Armoured Corps and also the Parachute Regiment, was killed in action on 24 March 1945, aged 22. He had been awarded the MBE just prior to his death on 27 February 'in recognition of gallant and distinguished services in the field'. He was the son of Edward Arthur and Marion McCulloch England of Great Yarmouth, Norfolk. He is buried in the Reichswald Forest War Cemetery in Germany.

Edward Anthony Jack Farrow, Sergeant (Air Gunner) 3005547, 158 Squadron, Royal Air Force Volunteer Reserve died on 3 March 1945 when his Halifax Bomber PN437 NP-X took off from Yorkshire at 1830hrs and crashed at Sledmere Grange, Yorkshire, killing all seven crew. They were headed for an oil refinery at Kamen. He was the son of Cecil and Dora Farrow of Aldeby, Norfolk. He is buried in the churchyard of St Mary's in Aldeby.

Arthur Harbour, Private 13095695 Pioneer Corps, died on 12 March 1945, aged 41. He was the son of Alfred and Gertrude Harbour and the husband of Pansy S. Harbour, all of Castle Acre where he is buried in the graveyard of St James Church.

Eric Charles Hemmant, Sergeant (Air Gunner) 3000858, 100 Squadron, Royal Air Force Volunteer Reserve, died 1 February

Crew inside a Halifax.

Cutaway of a Halifax bomber at the Science Museum, London.

1945, aged 22. He was the son of Harold and Ida Hemmant of Downham Market, Norfolk. He is buried in Durnbach War Cemetery, Germany.

Samuel Stephen Hewitt, Leading Aircraftman 1637004, Royal Air Force Volunteer Reserve, died 30 January 1946, aged 23. He was the son of Stephen Henry and Harriett Frances Hewitt, of Thornham, Norfolk and husband of Doris Renee Hewitt of Boston, Lincolnshire. He is buried in Kranji War Cemetery, Singapore.

Kenneth Basil Howlett, Private 14631679, 2nd Royal Norfolk Regiment, died 16 March 1945, aged 19. He was the son of William and Annie Howlett of Wymondham, Norfolk and had been an employee at CWS Brush works. He is buried at Taukkyan War Cemetery and commemorated on Wymondham War Memorial.

Douglas Frederick Hunter, Signalman 3778844, 2nd Division Signals, Royal Corps of Signals, died 27 February 1945, aged 31. He was the son of Mr and Mrs Frederick Walter Hunter and husband of Alice Maude Hunter of Downham Market, Norfolk. He is commemorated on Rangoon Memorial, Myanmar.

Dick Kemp, Stoker, 1st Class C/KX 127417 HMS *Goodall*, Royal Navy died 29 April 1945 when his ship was sunk by torpedo from *U-286* in the last U-boat attack of the war. He was aged 34 and the son of Albert and Ellen Kemp of Diss, Norfolk. He is commemorated on Chatham Naval Memorial, Kent.

Jack Stanley Lincoln, Private, 1st Battalion, Royal Norfolk Regiment, died 1 March 1945 in the liberation of Europe. He was the husband of Beatrice Lincoln. He is buried in Reichswald Forest War Cemetery and commemorated on the Memorial in St Augustine Church, Norwich, Norfolk.

Appendix 1

Norfolk Airfields in the Second World War

Some airfields were temporary and some were decoys. Among the major sites are the following:

RAF Attlebridge is 8 miles north-west of Norwich.

RAF Barton Bendish is situated opposite its parent station, RAF Marham.

RAF Bircham Newton. This base, 13 miles north of King's Lynn, was used in the Great War also.

RAF Bodney. This airbase is 5 miles south-west of Watton.

RAF Coltishall is 9 miles north-east of Norwich.

RAF Docking. Initially this was used as a decoy airfield for Bircham Newton with dummy Hudsons and, later, Hurricanes. Later, both the RAF and Royal Canadian Air force used the airfield.

RAF Downham Market.

RAF East Wretham, 6 miles north of Thetford, was the home of 311 (Czech) Squadron.

RAF Feltwell is located 10 miles west of Thetford.

RAF Fersfield. This was built in 1943/44 and is located 16 miles south-west of Norwich. The secret 'Operation Carthage' was launched from here on 21 March 1945, which raided the Shellhuset, Gestapo Headquarters in Copenhagen where dossiers were kept and Danish citizens tortured. It was deemed successful despite loss of civilian life.

RAF Foulsham. This airfield is 15 miles north-west of Norwich.

Shellhuset Gestapo Headquarters, Copenhagen, before and following the bombing.

RAF Great Massingham is situated 11.7 miles east of King's Lynn.

RAF Horsham St Faith. This is now Norwich International Airport.

RAF Langham. The most northerly of wartime RAF bases, being just over 3 miles from Blakeney.

RAF Little Snoring. This airfield was completed in late summer 1942.

RAF Ludham is Norfolk's most easterly airfield.

RAF Marham was originally a Great War base.

RAF Matlaske. An existing airfield was requisitioned by the Air Ministry in August 1939 and it became operational in October 1940 when it acted as a satellite to RAF Coltishall, 11 miles distant.

RAF Oulton. This airfield is 3 miles west of Aylsham.

RAF Sculthorpe. This airfield, 3 miles west of Fakenham, became operational in January 1943.

RAF Swanton Morley. This base is located 3 miles from Dereham and 18 miles north-west of Norwich.

RAF Watton. Opened just before the war, the first squadrons to use the base were Nos 21, 34 and 82, basically flying Blenheims.

RAF Wendling opened in 1942 and was home to the US Air Forces Eighth Air Force 392nd Bombardment Group.

RAF West Raynham. Opened in April 1939, quite a few squadrons used the base throughout the war.

RAF Weybourne had a varied life, for instance, during 1941 the De Havilland DH-82B Queen Bee target drones were based here. All flying activity was stopped from July 1942. The Muckleburgh Collection, the largest private military museum in the UK, is situated nearby.

Castle Meadow, Norwich, late 1930s.

The same shot today.

Bibliography

Bodle, Peter, *Yank Bomber Boys in Norfolk* (Fonthill Media, 2014)

Bowman, Martin W., *World War II RAF Airfields in Norfolk* (Pen and Sword Aviation, 2007)

Brooks, Peter F., *Coastal Towns at War* (Poppyland, 1988)

Burton, Lt Col. Reginald, *Railway of Hell* (Pen and Sword, 2010)

Docherty, Tom, *Dinghy Drop* (Pen and Sword Aviation, 2007)

Douglas Brown, R., *East Anglia 1939* (Terence Dalton, 1980)

Douglas Brown, R., *East Anglia 1940* (Terence Dalton, 1981)

Douglas Brown, R., *East Anglia 1941* (Terence Dalton, 1986)

Douglas Brown, R., *East Anglia 1942* (Terence Dalton, 1988)

Douglas Brown, R., *East Anglia 1943* (Terence Dalton, 1990)

Douglas Brown, R., *East Anglia 1944* (Terence Dalton, 1992)

Douglas Brown, R., *East Anglia 1945* (Terence Dalton, 1994)

Hart, Peter, *The 2nd Norfolk Regiment: From Le Paradis to Kohima* (Pen and Sword, 2011)

James, Derek, and EDP, *Norwich in the Blitz* (Archant, 2002)

Johnson, Derek E., *East Anglia at War 1939-45* (Jarrold, 1978)

Kent, Peter, *First and Second World War Coastal Defences* (Norfolk Museums Service)

Meeres, Frank, *Norfolk in the Second World War* (Phillimore, 2006)

Meeres, Frank, *Norfolk at War: Wings of Friendship* (Amberley, 2012)

Murell, C.N., *Dunkirk to the Rhineland* (Pen and Sword, 2011)

Rothnie, Niall, *The Baedeker Blitz* (Ian Allan, 1992)

Saunders, Andy, *Finding the Few* (Grub Street, 2013)

Smith, Graham, *Norfolk Airfields in the Second World War* (Countryside Books, 1994)

Snelling, Steve, *Norwich: A Shattered City* (Halsgrove, 2012)

Stephen, Dr Martin, *Poetry and Myths of the Great War* (Pen and Sword, 2014)

Wynn, Kenneth G., *Men of the Battle of Britain: A Biographical Directory of the Few* (Frontline Books, 2015)

The Maids Head Hotel and the Samson and Hercules, Norwich, today. During the war this quarter of town was a favourite of American troops who crowded into the hotel and ballroom at weekends. The legendary Glenn Miller played in the Samson and Hercules on 18 August 1944 – earlier in the day he had given a free concert from the bandstand at Chapelfield Gardens (see photo on page 15).

Index

A Short Guide to Great
    Britain, 128
Acle, 101, 239
Abdy Beauclerk, 29
Adair, Hubert 'Paddy', 70
Admiral Hipper, 90, 92
Admiral Scheer, 90
Agriculture, 10, 73, 167
Agricultural Hall, Norwich,
    26
Air Training Corps, 111, 166
Aldeburgh, 29
Aliens, round up of, 33, 52
At a Glance, events Local,
    World, 1, 32, 82, 125, 194,
    241, 293
Amenities ships, 287
America, 3, 38, 73, 106–107,
    132–3, 165, 168, 182, 184,
    257, 259, 311
Amphetamines and German
    troops, 229
Anderson, Sir John, 23
Andrewsfield, 201
Anglo-German Naval Treaty,
    2
Anglo-Soviet friendship, 116
Ark Royal, HMS, 85
Arnhem, 243, 282
Assembly Rooms, Norwich,
    26

Attleborough, 22, 183, 246
Attlebridge, 305
AVIVA, 14
Aylsham, 22, 24, 250, 307

Bader, Douglas, 61, 68, 70,
    73, 86, 110, 112
Baedeker Blitz, 126, 146
Bailey, H.F., 92, 94, 163
Barcelona, 1
Barclay, George DFC, 71
Barnards, 58, 87
Barton Bendish, 305
Barton, Joe VC, 245
Bates, Sidney (Basher) VC,
    268–9
Battle of Britain, 59–70
Beaverbrook, Lord, 74
Belgium, 32, 44–6, 85, 242–3,
    271, 277
Belsen, Allies enter, 295
Berlin, Battle of, Attacks on,
    34, 197, 206, 210, 237,
    297–8
Big Week, The, 241, 255
'Big Wing' concept, 69
Bircham Newton, 95, 305
Bismarck, 84, 90–1, 117, 120
'Black Thursday', 197, 211
Blackout, 7, 26, 36, 86, 95,
    294

Blakeney, 207, 307
Blenheim (aircraft), 21, 110, 307
Blogg, Henry, 90, 93
Bodney, 201, 223
Bond, R.H., 14, 159, 238
Bouch, Sam, 226
    see also, Tungate, Albert
Boulton & Paul, 13, 58, 73, 74, 86, 91
Boxted, 201
Bracondale, Norwich, 86, 157
Bremen and the Royal Norfolks, 209–10, 299
British Legion and Home Guard eligibility, 289
British Expeditionary Force (BEF), 26, 46
British Restaurants, 104–105
Buchenwald, US troops enter, 296
Burial Clubs, 16
Burma, 128, 213, 215–16
Burton, Montague, 14
Bussey, Sam, 157

Caen, assault on, 264–5
Caine, Sir Michael, 99
Caley, A.J., 13–14, 48
Casablanca Conference, 203
Castle Camps, 58, 147
Chamberlain, Neville, 20, 42
Chipping Ongar, 201
Chungkai, 213
Colman's mustard, 13–14
Conscientious objectors, 53, 162

Corfu, HMS, 302
Czechoslovakia, 2

D-Day, 263–5
    see also Operation Overlord
Darsham, 26
Debden, 62, 65
Decoy sites, 95
Deenethorpe, 201
Denmark, invasion of, 45
Docking, 43
Downham Market, 12
Dresden, bombing of, 298
Dunkirk, 45–50
Duxford, 68, 95

Eaker, Gen, 203, 210
Eddingtons 14
Eder Dam, destruction of, 207
    see also Mohne Dam, destruction of
Edrich, Bill, 110
Eisenhower, Gen Dwight, 198, 259
El Alamein, 187, 216
Elsdon, Thomas 'Jimmie' DFC, OBE, 71
Emergency Powers (Defence) Bill, 6
Eye, 201

Falaise Pocket, The, 269–71
Food at Home, Recipes, 167–72

see also Food for the troops, Recipes

Food for the troops, 228–30
see also Food at home, Recipes, Prices

Formby, George, 22, 50

France, Fall of, 86
see also France, Liberation of

France, Liberation of, 263–5
see also France, Fall of

French Resistance/Maquis, 56

Gas Masks, Precautions, 21, 41, 52, 73

Gimbert, Benjamin GC, 24

Gneisenau, 81, 129

Goering, Hermann, 64, 69, 204

Gristock, Sgt Maj George VC, 47

Grix, John David, 146, 161

Gypsy, HMS, 29

Hamburg, Battle of, 206

Handley, Tommy, 50

Happisburgh, 20, 29, 52

Harleston, 22

Harris, ACM Sir Arthur, 162, 206, 210, 295–6, 298

Harwich, 3, 29, 45, 57, 61, 64

Haw Haw, Lord, 56, 141

Hawker Hurricane, 60

Haybox, 167, 173

Hereward, HMS, 45–6

Hess, Rudolf, 84, 107

Hiroshima, 295, 301
see also Nagasaki

Hichens, Lt Cdr Robert, DSO, DSC, 226

Holkham, 101

Holland, fall of, 33, 45, 50

Home Guard, 15, 36, 55–6, 78, 97, 130, 165, 236, 243, 289

Honington, 43, 65

Horsham St Faiths, Norwich, 57, 65, 110, 184–5, 201–202, 223, 256, 307

Humphreys, Peter DFC, 72

Hunter, Lt D. Lee, 258

Hurricane (aircraft), 21, 57, 60–2, 64–5, 69, 71, 73, 79, 80, 86, 110, 305

Ice-cream, public demand for in 1944/5, 243, 288–9

Ijmuiden, 207, 225–6

Imphal, 242, 258–60, 291

Invasion exercises and plans, 84, 96, 131

Ironside, Gen, 55

Italian prisoners, 127, 167, 221, 234, 244, 277
see also German prisoners of war

Jamieson, Capt David VC, 267

Jewish community, 221, 223

Jobs and pay, 10, 12–13, 17, 112, 129, 278

'Julius Caesar' codename, 44

Kennedy, Joseph P., Jnr, 276
    see also Lieutenant
        Wilford J. Willy
Ketteringham Hall, 202
King George V, HMS, 91
King Edward VII Grammar
    School, King's Lynn, 101,
    137
Knettishall, 201, 210
Knowland, Arthur VC, 300
Kohima, assault of, 258–60
Krushchev, Nikita, 230

Land Girls, 101, 122
Laurence, Scott &
    Electromotors Ltd, 13, 86
Leigh, Arthur 'Joe' DFM
    DFC, 72
Lend-Lease Bill, 34, 83, 106,
    297
Le Paradis Massacre, 49–50
Le Pont de la Riviere Kwai,
    Pierre Boulle, 215
Lexham, 178, 181
Lifeboats, rescues, 29, 43, 90,
    92–3, 133, 162–3
Little Snoring, 182, 307
Ludham, 307
Luxembourg, 33, 44, 243

Maas, battle for, 279, 282,
    293, 299
Magee, John, 109–10
'Make do and Mend', 173,
    178

Maquis, 56–7
March (town), 58
Marham, 43, 69, 95, 194,
    203–204, 305
Martlesham, 22, 59, 61–2, 64,
    86, 95, 110–11, 201
Mass Observation, 76, 100,
    221
Memorials, 155, 246–52
Metfield, 201
Methwold, 205, 207
Mighty Eighth, 255
Mildenhall, 44, 95
Mohne Dam, destruction of,
    206–207
    see also Eder Dam,
        destruction of
Montgomery, Gen Bernard,
    187, 194, 198, 217–18, 260,
    264–5, 282, 298–9
Morrison shelter, 90
Mosley, Sir Oswald, 52
Mountbatten, Lord Louis,
    197, 216, 295, 301
Mundesley, 53, 80, 120, 192,
    227, 275
Mustang (aircraft), 298
Mutual Aid Good
    Neighbours' Association
    (MAGNA), 161

Nagasaki, 295, 301–302
    see also Hiroshima
National Union of
    Agricultural Workers, 166,
    278

Netherlands, 45, 46, 86, 219, 238, 297
see also Queen Wilhelmina
Nightall, William GC, 245, 252
Nisbet, J. Cooper, 43
Non-Combatant Corps, 52, 54
Nore Command, 225
Norfolk Air Raids (ARP) Committee, 22
Norfolk and Norwich Hospital, 26, 158
North Walsham, 22, 24
Norway, fall of, 33, 45, 50, 86, 125
Norwich Grammar School, 10
Nuremberg, bombing of, 252

Observer Corps, 61
Old Buckenham, and Museum, 158, 183, 201
Old Catton, 202
Operation 'Overlord', 197, 235, 259, 261
see also D-Day
Operation 'Starkey', 236
Ordre National de la Légion d'Honneur, 271
Orne Crossing, 267

Paddy Hendly, 92
Pas de Calais, 110, 264–5
Patton, Gen George S., 267–8
Pearl Harbor, 85, 106, 116

Peenemunde, attack on, 196, 210
Pickard, Group Capt Percy DSO, 255–7
Pie scheme, 196
Polish community in Norfolk, 136, 223
PoW Associations, 234
Prices, 12–16
see also Shopping
Prinz Eugen, 90
Prince of Wales, HMS, 85, 91, 95, 117
Prisoner of War Week, 176

Radio Direction-Finding (RDF) Stations, 24
Radio Oranje, 46, 47
Railway of Death, 212–13
Randle, Capt John N. VC, 258
Rationing, Ration books, 7, 27–8, 33, 38, 86, 104, 130, 167, 173, 296–7
Raydon, 201
Repulse, HMS, 85
Rhur, Battle of, 299
Richthofen, Baron Von (Red Baron), 13
Ridgewell, 201, 212, 252
Robertson, Frederick DFM, 72–3
Rommel, FM Erwin, 82, 84, 116, 128, 187, 217, 265
Roosevelt, President Franklin D., 36, 84, 106, 127, 179, 194, 196–7, 203, 230, 243, 293

Royal Norfolk Regiment, 49, 77, 81, 116, 177, 213, 238–9, 258, 292, 300, 303

Royan, Allied bombing of, 298

Runton, East and West, 262

Rushmer, Frederick 'Rusty', 73

'Salute the Soldier' Week, 244

Scharnhorst, 81, 125, 129, 218, 220

Schnellboot, 132, 226

Scout and Guide movement, 23, 78, 232, 234

Seething, 201

Sexual matters, 234–5
  see also Venereal Disease

Shelters, 2, 6, 22, 24, 26, 141

Shipdham, 184, 198, 204, 209–10

Simon Bolivar, 29

Singapore, Fall of, 129, 212–13, 286–7

Snettisham, 30, 291

Sopwith Camel (aircraft), 14, 74, 91

Southwold, 43, 235

Spam, 230

Spitfire (aircraft), 19, 21, 43, 57, 59–61, 64, 72–3, 110, 132, 274

Sprowston, Norwich, 58

SS Panzer Corps, 265

Stanford Battle Area, 184–7

Steeple Morden, 201

Stirling (bomber), 162, 202, 239

St Nicholas Great Yarmouth, Church of, 134, 138–40, 251

Stoke Holy Cross 26

St Peter Mancroft, Church of, 74, 145–6, 155, 289–90

Stradishall, 44

Strangers, 99, 219–24

Swaffham, 12, 104, 239

Swanton Morley, 184, 298, 307

Teichman, Sir Eric, murder of, 245

Territorial Army, 2–5, 44

Terukuni Maru, 29

Thatcher, Margaret, 230

Thorpe Abbots, 201

Thompson, F. Longstreth, 237

Tibenham, 158, 201

Tobruk, 84–5, 126

Townsend, Sqd Ldr Peter, 61

Tungate, Albert, 225
  see also Bouch, Sam

Tunis, victory parade, 218

U-boats, 6, 29, 195, 204

Umpire, HMS, 91

USAAF, 127, 182, 184, 194, 196–7, 199, 201, 207–208, 210–11, 244, 261, 267, 294, 298

Utility products, 165

V1s and V2s, 271–6
Venereal disease, 234–5
   see also Sexual Matters
Ventura (aircraft), 205, 207
Victoria Cross, 47–8, 245,
   258, 269, 301
Vortigern, HMS, 132, 135

'Warship Weeks', 173
Warspite, HMS, 265
Wells, 75, 93, 101, 225
Wendling, 201, 307
Wellington (aircraft), 21,
   69–70, 93, 162
Weybourne, 96, 307
Wiesbaden, attack on, 297
Wilhelmina, Queen, 45–7
   see also Netherlands

Willy, Lt Wilford J., 276
   see also Kennedy, Joseph
   P Jnr
Winfarthing-Fersfield Army
   Base, 276
Wood, Sir Kingsley, 176
Woolton, Lord, 168, 232
Women, new roles for, 10, 55,
   64, 100, 103, 111, 165, 167,
   231
Woodward, James, 113

Yanks, 178

Zeppelins, 10, 23, 28, 275
Zero Stations, 57
'Zoning', 221